TURBOCHARGED!

100 Simple Secrets to Successful Preschool Ministry

Group

Loveland, Colorado

group.com

Group resources actually work!

This Group resource incorporates our R.E.A.L. approach to ministry. It reinforces a growing friendship with Jesus, encourages long-term learning, and results in life transformation, because it's

Relational
Learner-to-learner interaction enhances learning and builds Christian friendships.

Experiential
What learners experience through discussion and action sticks with them up to 9 times longer than what they simply hear or read.

Applicable
The aim of Christian education is to equip learners to be both hearers and doers of God's Word.

Learner-based
Learners understand and retain more when the learning process takes into consideration how they learn best.

Turbocharged!: 100 Simple Secrets to Successful Preschool Ministry
Copyright © 2009 Group Publishing, Inc.

Visit our website: **group.com**

Credits
Contributing Authors: Eric Echols, Gina Franzke, Dale Hudson, and Barbara Price
Cover and Illustrations: Matt Wood

Unless otherwise indicated, all Scripture quotations are taken from the *Holy Bible*, New Living Translation, copyright © 1996, 2004, 2007. Used by permission of Tyndale House Publishers, Inc., Carol Stream, Illinois 60188. All rights reserved.

Library of Congress Cataloging-in-Publication Data
Hudson, Dale, 1967-

Turbocharged! : 100 simple secrets to successful preschool ministry / [Dale Hudson ... et al.]. -- 1st American pbk. ed.
      p. cm.
  ISBN 978-0-7644-4003-8 (pbk. : alk. paper)
 1. Church work with children. I. Hudson, Dale, 1967-
  BV639.C4H79 2009
  259'.22--dc22
                                            2009042060

10 9 8 7 6 5 4 3 2 1   18 17 16 15 14 13 12 11 10 09

Printed in the United States of America.

CONTENTS

Preschool Ministry Environment

Preschool Ministry Volunteers

Preschoolers' Parents

Preschool Ministry Leadership & Vision

INTRODUCTION

This weekend I'll have the privilege of baptizing a fourth-grader who attends our church. She loves Jesus with all her heart. In fact, she recently started a Bible club on her own called "That's the Spirit." She chose the name to reflect how God's Spirit is working in her life.

When she was 3 years old and the family wasn't attending church, this precious girl asked to go. Finally her mother succumbed to her daughter's pleas and took her to church. After a few years, the family was reached and their lives were changed...and it all began with God working in the heart of a preschooler.

Studies show that we become much of who we are in our preschool years. A child's spiritual formation begins in this critical, formative stage of life. We must be equipped and passionate about preschool ministry!

This book is all about helping you reach and minister to preschoolers and their families. The strategies, ideas, and philosophies you're about to read flow from hands-on preschool ministry experience. We've seen them work, and we believe they can work for your ministry as well. Go through this book with your team. Have open discussions and strategize together about how to take your preschool ministry to a new level.

A healthy, growing preschool ministry is a great indicator of a church that's healthy and growing. To put it plainly...a turbocharged preschool ministry will result in a turbocharged church and turbocharged families.

We thank God for you and your heart for preschoolers and their families. May he infuse your life and ministry with a fresh touch, new vision, and creative strategies. We believe with you that your best days of preschool ministry are just around the corner!

Dale Hudson
Director of Children's Ministries
Christ Fellowship Church
Palm Beach Gardens, Florida

Preschoolers: Who Are They?

1

What Every Preschooler Needs From Your Team!

Preschoolers need 11 things from your ministry team—put them all together and they spell *preschooler*.

Prayer—Nothing of eternal value will be accomplished in preschoolers' lives without prayer. God can do more in seconds than we can do in a lifetime.

- Pray regularly for the preschoolers in your ministry.
- Encourage your team to pray through their preschool ministry rosters.
- Pray with the children each weekend.
- Teach the children to pray. Some of the sweetest, most genuine prayers that have ever been uttered came from preschoolers.
- Call parents and ask them how you can pray for their children.
- Put a prayer verse on the wall in each preschool room—a unique prayer for this year in a child's life. Pray it each week for the children in that room.

Recognition—Every child wants to be known and to know that he or she is valued. Preschoolers need to be recognized and called by name. Learn children's names and use them. Every week find at least one good thing to recognize about each child and acknowledge it.

Eye Contact—Children need to be looked in the eye when engaged in conversation to feel you're genuinely interested in them. This usually means getting down to preschoolers' eye level.

Security—Preschoolers are growing up in a scary world. Parents hold them closely for fear of kidnapping, abuse, or endangerment. Church must be a safe place. Go the second mile to make sure every team member has been background-checked, interviewed, reference-checked, and approved.

Have a thoroughly secure check-in and check-out system. Put in place volunteer procedures and policies that provide security.

Care—Even at their young ages, preschoolers can sense when someone genuinely cares for them. They need leaders who'll care enough to pray for their boo-boos, send them "miss you" cards when they're absent, and cheer for them at their kindergarten graduations.

Happy Birthday—Birthdays are a big deal for preschoolers. They need you to celebrate their special day—so sing, bring in a birthday treat, and give a small gift to the birthday child.

Opportunity—Preschoolers need the opportunity to hear God's truth and build a foundation for faith development.

Open Ears—Every child needs someone who'll listen with open ears. So really listen...to preschoolers' stories, questions, fears, and small talk.

Laughter—Every preschooler needs to be able to laugh...to have fun...to be able to be a child. Preschoolers need leaders who'll encourage this through age-appropriate activities that allow laughter to happen spontaneously.

Empowerment—God has given each preschooler unique talents and abilities. Empower your preschoolers to use these talents and abilities through learning experiences and activities where they can succeed.

Rules—Preschoolers need clear rules to follow, accompanied with firm and loving guidance, opportunities to make choices, and consistent consequences.

—**Dale**

2

Watch Me Grow

I keep a photo of my youngest daughter just above my workspace at church. It was taken at vacation Bible school when she was 3 years old. She's praying to Jesus with her hands folded and her eyes squeezed shut. The look on her face speaks of a determination for God to do something great. It's as if she's praying for true revival to break out. More than likely that wasn't on her mind. All I know is that every time I look at it, I'm filled with complete joy. After I take in the expression on her face, though, the next thing I notice is that she's wearing her princess shoes—and then I burst into laughter. I wanted her to stay 3 forever.

My favorite thing about preschool ministry is getting to be around 3-year-olds every week. Have you ever noticed how happy they are just to be here? When I'm having a bad day, I think, *Go visit the 3-year-old ministry, and all things miserable will vanish.* When I come to the door, they run to get hugs and receive my words of praise.

As precious as they are, though, teaching them can be frustrating if you don't know what they're capable of doing. Here are developmental characteristics common in 3-year-olds.

- **Preschoolers play with other children.** This is different from 2-year-olds, who play alongside other children. Three-year-olds need to know the names of the other kids. Help them meet and make new friends.

- **Preschoolers are very active.** Playtime is essential for large muscle development. Give them lots of opportunities to run, jump, tumble, and climb.

- **Preschoolers' fine motor skills have developed.** They're able to color with more ease and pick up small objects. Not all 3-year-olds are ready for scissors, but crayons or markers are perfect for helping them hone their fine motor skills.

- **Preschoolers are very imaginative.** Let them use their imaginations, especially during Bible time. Three-year-olds love to pretend they're in the lion's den or in the belly of a giant fish.

- **Preschoolers like to listen to books and look at pictures.** Use pictures to help convey spiritual concepts or biblical truth.

- **Preschoolers have short attention spans.** Don't worry about 3-year-olds who don't seem to be listening. Often they're learning more than those who seem to be engaged.

- **Preschoolers want to please adults, and they thrive on approval.** Shower them with genuine praise over every little thing. This also builds confidence.

- **Preschoolers are sensitive.** Use a calm, loving voice when talking. Saying something with the wrong tone or voice inflection could upset them.

- **Preschoolers have increased self-control.** Three-year-olds know right from wrong and what obedience is. Help them continue to function within the rules.

- **Preschoolers ask lots of questions.** This is how they learn. Don't let it drive you crazy; be patient.

- **Preschoolers like making their own choices.** Let them choose the play centers or color of crayons they want to use. Offer activity options. They'll grow as they confidently make choices.

- **Preschoolers are just beginning to learn how to share.** Role-play sharing with them while they're playing.

Three-year-olds are wonderful. Get to know who 3-year-olds are so you can better teach them about who God is.

—**Gina**

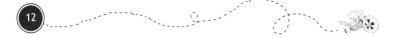

Look at Me

I'm not a big fan of roller coasters, but for the sake of living up to being a "fun mom," I endure them. If I had to pick a favorite ride, it would be the Rock 'n' Roller Coaster at Walt Disney World. It goes from 0 to 60 in 2.8 seconds. The one and only time I rode it, I was lucky enough to get in the first car—it's a minute and 22 seconds of pure excitement.

The Rock 'n' Roller Coaster offers a great illustration of the way children grow and develop during the first four years of their lives. From a baby's first breath, he or she takes off on a rapid-pace journey of learning and exploration. It's like going from 0 to 60 in 2.8 seconds.

As preschoolers mature, their growth rate begins to slow down. Around 4 years of age, preschoolers start to refine the skills they've learned during the first four years of their lives. They're ready to show you how big they really are and what they can accomplish on their own. When teaching older preschoolers, 4 and 5 years old, knowing their developmental characteristics will help you be more effective.

- **Older preschoolers' social skills continue to grow and develop.** Give them opportunities to socialize with one another.

- **Older preschoolers are learning to respect others.** They're ready for rules, so set guidelines they can follow; for example, be kind to one another, share your toys, and listen to your leaders.

- **Older preschoolers are learning to share.** Remind them that sharing pleases Jesus and that everyone can have a turn.

- **Older preschoolers' small muscles are continuing to develop.** They're more capable of cutting out shapes and are able to color within the lines. Four- and 5-year-olds are ready for scissors, but make sure they're not sharp or pointed. Cutting out shapes and crafts gives kids a great sense of independence.

- **Like 3-year-olds, older preschoolers want to please adults, and they thrive on approval.** Shower them with genuine praise, and let them know how proud you are of them.

- **Older preschoolers enjoy and want more responsibility.** Make a list of chores they can do in your room; for example, scooting chairs up to the tables, sweeping the floor, wiping down the tables, and picking up toys.

- **Older preschoolers want to make choices.** Let them choose a play center or craft experience.

- **Older preschoolers need climbing apparatuses and active play to release energy.** If you have access to outside play, take advantage of that. If not, make sure you include some energy-busting activities within your schedule.

- **Older preschoolers are curious.** Four- and 5-year-olds ask lots of questions. You may even need to plan an extra five to 10 minutes of group time just so you can answer all their questions. Have fun with this and understand that this is how older preschoolers learn.

- **Older preschoolers can express themselves well and show their feelings of anger and happiness.** Be prepared for emotional outbursts, but never respond with a raised voice. As Proverbs tells us, "A gentle answer deflects anger, but harsh words make tempers flare."

An important thing to remember about 4- and 5-year-olds is that, although they're becoming more independent and doing more things on their own, they still need our help. It's easy to get impatient with older preschoolers, especially when they've been going along doing things for themselves and then all of a sudden they have a little bump in the road. Adults and parents need to demonstrate patience. The way you react and respond to children's needs will affect the development of their self-esteem and self-confidence.

Your older preschoolers are at a critical time of development in their lives. They're finally beginning to put it all together. How exciting for you as a preschool leader to know that you play a vital role as you assist them in this learning process. Give them the love, kindness, and patience they need as they grow toward fulfilling God's purpose for their lives.

—Gina

Without a doubt, boys and girls learn differently. Gender differences are very real, present at birth, and a critical factor in how a child is raised, disciplined, and educated. This doesn't mean that all girls learn one way and all boys another, but there are significant differences that appear to be at their highest level among preschool children. Check out these differing areas.

Hearing—This is one of the earliest differences that can be documented. Girls can hear soft sounds better than boys. This difference alone can cause problems in your preschool ministry. If an adult speaks in a normal tone of voice at the front of the room, boys at the back of the room may not pay attention simply because they can't hear what's being said.

Rate of physical and mental maturity—Another difference that's obvious to even the most casual observer is that girls mature physically and mentally faster than boys. By the age of 6, girls can be one year ahead of boys. A boy will probably not be able to write as well as a same-age girl because muscle development in girls' hands is more advanced.

Behavior issues—Adults tend to reprimand boys more harshly and more often than girls, which can lead to increased aggressiveness in boys. This directly relates to the fact that boys are tested for learning and behavioral disorders twice as often as girls and represent two-thirds of children who'll repeat a grade. The increasing number of boys being diagnosed with attention-deficit hyperactivity disorder might actually be a result of teaching that ignores gender differences.

How we approach these gender differences can enhance our education practices, minimize discipline problems, and create a more productive, gender-friendly learning atmosphere. To make your preschool ministry more gender appropriate, take inborn differences into consideration when developing programs.

Because gender differences are at their strongest in early childhood, we can't put boys and girls into the same room and expect them to learn in the same manner. Consider making these suggested small changes to create a friendly environment for boys and girls.

- Have boys sit closer to you so they're able to hear you better.

- Give boys more time to answer questions because while girls' brains excel at memory, boys' brains are more task-focused. Boys are likely to withdraw if they feel overwhelmed or pressured.

- When engaging kids in singing, keep in mind that girls are six times more likely than boys to sing in tune at an early age.

- Adjust your visual environment. Boys' and girls' brains process images differently. Girls are more aware of color and texture; boys are better at discerning direction and speed. Also, keep your room lighting bright because boys tend to struggle if lighting is too dim.

- When serving snacks, keep in mind that there's a gender difference in taste. Girls prefer sweet snacks, while boys prefer salty foods.

- Add movement to preschool ministry. Movement helps stimulate boys' brains and manage their impulsive behavior. Discipline problems with boys can often be avoided by allowing them to keep their hands busy while learning.

—**Barbara**

Now I Lay Me Down to Sleep

Certain prayers recited at mealtime and bedtime have been passed down from generation to generation for centuries. Our parents and grandparents taught many of us these simple prayers when we were preschool age. The most recited prayer before mealtime is "God is great! God is good! Let us thank him for our food." And at bedtime: "Now I lay me down to sleep, I pray the Lord my soul to keep; and if I die before I wake, I pray the Lord my soul to take." Apparently the pronunciation of "good" and "food" rhymed at one time, and nothing says "sweet dreams" like a prayer about dying in your sleep.

These prayers are frequently used to introduce children to the idea of communicating with God, but preschoolers can learn to talk to God about more than eating and sleeping. Instead of rote prayers, we can teach parents and preschoolers to speak to God as a friend by using simple, conversational language. In our preschool ministry, we help kids move beyond memorized prayers to talking to God in their own words by asking two questions, "What do you want to thank God for?" and "How do you want God to help you?"

Thank you, God, for... We teach preschoolers to have an attitude of gratitude by teaching them to thank God for what's occurred in their day. This helps them understand "Whatever is good and perfect comes down to us from God our Father" (James 1:17). For young children, thankfulness flows from a natural expression of devotion and love. By teaching little ones to be thankful, we're showing them the many ways God loves them and how to express their love and devotion back to God.

Walk-around prayer—A practical way to teach kids to be thankful is to walk around your preschool classroom and point out things you're thankful for. Turn it into a prayer of thanks by saying, "Thank you, God, for..." and naming each of the things you're thankful for. Then have preschoolers do the same.

Thank you box—Have kids help you decorate a special thank you box. Each week, have one of the children take the box home and place an item inside that he or she is thankful for. Then next week during your prayer time, open the box and have the child tell about what he or she is thankful for.

God, help me... When preschoolers are taught to ask God for help, they learn to be dependent on God. They learn they need his help to live by the principles in his Word. We teach young children that they need God's help to obey their parents, forgive their siblings, and be all God wants them to be. By asking for help, they learn that God is trustworthy. It also reminds them that God is concerned with every detail of their lives.

How do we build the practice of asking God for help into our preschool ministry?

Role model—The first way to help preschoolers is to model it. For example, at times all children have difficulty sharing; when this occurs, take a moment to pray with those involved and ask God for help.

Prayer circle—Have preschoolers sit in a circle, and ask children to each name one thing they'd like God's help with this week. Write down their prayer requests, and follow up the next week to see how God worked.

Prayer is foundational for every preschooler's relationship with God. It's preschoolers' way to access God; it teaches them dependency on God and develops their faith. We can teach preschoolers to talk to God in their own way with confidence that God hears them. Encourage your children to move beyond rote prayers by asking God for help and thanking God for what he's done.

—**Eric**

Kids Are So Smart

God loves variety. Think of all the wonderful varieties of plants, animals, colors, and fish God created. Think about all the different types of people God created. It would be boring if we were all the same. God also created preschoolers with multiple intelligences—intrinsic ways that they're smart and that they learn best.

The effective preschool ministry recognizes this and seeks to engage all the multiple intelligences.

Word-smart preschoolers are sensitive to the meaning and order of words. They use an expanded vocabulary. They respond to jokes, riddles, reading, writing, storytelling, and word games.

Logic-smart preschoolers like reasoning, patterns, and order. They want to know how things work, ask lots of questions, and collect things. They respond to puzzles, blocks, and counting devices.

Body-smart preschoolers enjoy sports and physical activity. They respond to body language, dance, acting, and active games.

Music-smart preschoolers are sensitive to pitch, melody, rhythm, and tone. They love to listen to and play music, sing, hum, move to rhythm, and create tunes.

Picture-smart preschoolers perceive the world accurately and recreate or transform aspects of that world. They like puzzles, mazes, doodling, painting, drawing, building with blocks, and taking things apart and putting them back together again.

Nature-smart preschoolers recognize and classify the numerous species of an environment. They like to spend time outdoors observing plants, collecting rocks, and catching insects. They love nature.

People-smart preschoolers are all about people and relationships. They have many friends; they're good mediators and team players. They enjoy group games and discussions.

Self-smart preschoolers use their emotional life to understand themselves and others. They control their feeling and emotions. They do a lot of observing and listening. They do best when working alone. They enjoy journals and reflective questions about their experiences and emotions.

Whenever you create a lesson for preschoolers, consider all the ways that kids are smart. Over the course of a few lessons, you should hit all of them to reach all kids where they're already intelligent.

Here's an example. Let's take Jonah and the Big Fish (Jonah 1-2).

Word Smart—Dramatically paraphrase the Bible passage to preschoolers; then have them retell it to someone else in the room.

Logic Smart—Have preschoolers put together a puzzle of Jonah and the the Big Fish.

Body Smart—Have them act out the Scripture.

Music Smart—Lead them in singing a song about Jonah and the Big Fish.

Picture Smart—Have them draw a picture of what happened in the Bible.

Nature Smart—Bring some seaweed for them to touch or a picture of a large fish for them to look at.

People Smart—Have them play a group game and discuss what happened with friends.

Self Smart—Ask them questions and have them draw pictures about how they would've felt if they were Jonah.

All of us have a tendency to teach out of our own learning style because it's our comfort zone. Challenge yourself and other preschool leaders to engage all of kids' smarts. When that happens, children will be excited about coming to church because they'll be learning the way they enjoy most.

—Dale

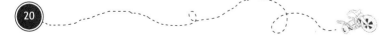

Separation anxiety is one of the toughest challenges for preschool ministry leaders and parents of preschoolers. For leaders, it disrupts the ministry and tends to spread like wildfire to the other children. For parents, it's frustrating and heartbreaking because no parent wants to see his or her child in distress. To deal with a child's unwillingness to leave a parent or caregiver, you need to understand why children go through this stage.

Separation anxiety is a sign that a child's beginning to understand his or her environment. When children can't see their parents, they exhibit anxious behaviors because they want their parents to stay close. Also, young children can't yet understand time, so they don't know when or even if their parents will be back. This is a normal and healthy part of psychological development. Separation anxiety usually begins at about 8 months of age, and children can still experience great fear of being separated from their parents when they're as old as 5 or 6.

Separation anxiety can be more intense when a child's experiencing a transition in life. There are times all children will experience difficult transitions. For example, when a child's intelligence has reached the level where he or she is able to recognize someone as a stranger, having this person near will make the child anxious. Also, changes a child may be experiencing at home can create insecurities. These circumstances could be events such as moving, a change in a day care situation, relationship problems between parents, or the arrival of a new sibling. If you're able to recognize major events in children's lives, your patience and understanding can help ease them through transitions.

Separation anxiety can be lessened with routines to help children feel secure. Have the parent establish a routine of hugs, kisses, and parting words. A familiar pattern will make it easier for a child to adjust. It also helps reassure children if the opening elements in your preschool ministry are consistent. Use the same songs, the same type of story, prayer, and so on.

A regular routine is a fundamental part of your preschool ministry; stay as consistent as possible when leaders and rooms change.

Separation anxiety must be addressed if it becomes severe. Be willing to acknowledge the problem if separation anxiety becomes serious. This can be judged by how intensely and how long the child cries. If the child cries uncontrollably for a long time and begins to show signs of anger, it's time to call the child's parent. There's no lesson worth putting a child—and the other children—through an hour of agony.

Here are the do's and don'ts for dealing with separation anxiety.

DO reassure parents that an adjustment period is normal and expected.

DON'T encourage a parent to sneak out when his or her child isn't looking. This leaves the child thinking the worst.

DO have the child bring an item such as a stuffed toy that he or she finds comforting.

DON'T have parents stay around waiting for their child to stop crying. This only prolongs the agony.

DO reassure a child that his or her parents will be back. Because children don't understand the concept of time, explain this in a way they'll understand such as, "Your parents will be back right after snack time."

DON'T scold. Separation anxiety isn't a discipline problem.

DO take children's anxieties seriously, and treat preschoolers with understanding, patience, and love.

—Barbara

Imagine That

Preschoolers are hard-wired for imagination. Any given Sunday, you may find yourself in a room with princesses, superheroes, or even the occasional Tyrannosaurus Rex. Some well-meaning preschool leaders say that we run a big risk when we allow the truth of the Bible to merge with the imagination of kids. They argue that preschoolers have a difficult time differentiating the truth of God's Word from fantasy and will begin to think of Jesus as a fictional character. But preschoolers are very capable of navigating between what's real and what's fantasy. In fact, when we capitalize on their ability to seamlessly move between the real world and fantasy, we can better minister to preschoolers.

Creatively teach God's Word. The Bible is the account of God's relationship with us. It's not boring, but we make it boring if we simply read it straight from our curriculum. So don't just read the Bible, tell it. Understand the concepts, study the principles in your curriculum, and then paint a picture for your preschoolers' imaginations by telling what happened in your own words.

Preschoolers will pay attention as long as their curiosity is engaged. Once they lose interest in what you're saying, they'll focus their attention on something else, such as snack time or when their parents are coming to pick them up.

Use music to enhance your ministry. Preschoolers love to dance and move to music. Encourage your kids to participate through singing, dancing, and playing homemade or toy instruments.

Use sound effects to engage the imagination of your preschoolers and enhance their experience of God's Word. Incorporate instrumental mood music to set the stage for the part of God's Bible you're exploring. Allow preschoolers to join you in making music by stomping feet, clapping hands, or rubbing their hands together.

Encourage pretend play. Children learn a lot from dramatizing events because it allows them to put themselves into the truth of what happened. So create a dress-up box with clothes and props gathered from local thrift stores, yard sales, and even your own closet and garage. Then allow your preschoolers to dress like the people in the Bible and act it out. Pretend play helps them to identify with people, understand the setting, and remember the action and sequence of events. Acting out the Bible in pretend play helps children comprehend what they've heard.

Unleash preschoolers' creativity. Put away the sterile coloring sheets and allow kids to create their own art projects. For most preschoolers, exploration of materials is the most important aspect of making art and unleashing their creativity. Avoid art projects that require too-fine motor skills; it's the process that's important, not the finished product. So as kids work with the supplies you've given them—water, clay, sand, dough, paints, papers, buttons, ribbons—respect the process. Don't worry if preschoolers don't create the exact replica of the craft; allow them the freedom to explore and express their artistic interpretation of what they're learning.

Scripture is clear that we're all created in God's image. God is creative and so are your preschoolers. Tap into their imaginations. Take them on a journey of exploration and discovery as you introduce their imaginations to the truth of Scripture.

—**Eric**

Small Talk

How do you carry on a conversation with a preschooler? Here are some tips to improve your "small talk."

Listen...it all starts with knowing how to listen to preschoolers.

At ages 2 to 3...

- kids begin to use complete sentences, think logically, and understand sequences of events.

- kids use the word *no* to claim their space; they use the word *why* to question authority and also as a way to engage in conversation.

- kids begin to make up their own explanations of things. For example, "When it rains, the sky is crying."

- kids like to imitate other people's words. You may hear them repeating words to their pets or toys that they heard someone else say. I remember doing this when I was in preschool. I had a Dennis the Menace toy. Any time I got in trouble, I turned around and gave him the same reprimand.

- kids like to hear about and describe the same event over and over again. This gives them a sense of security.

By ages 3 to 5...

- kids begin to understand cause and effect. For example, "If you drink your milk, you'll have strong bones."

- kids can reason out hypothetical situations, such as, "If this happened, what would you do?

- kids are more patient in conversation and more willing to take turns talking.

- kids also communicate through their body language, art, and play.

When you're in conversation with preschoolers...

- spend just as much time listening as you do talking.

- ask more than just yes or no questions. Ask open-ended questions to encourage them to talk.

- get down on their level. Lean or kneel down to make them feel more comfortable.

- look into their eyes. Show genuine interest in them.

- watch your tone; don't talk down to them. Let your tone reflect kindness.

- learn about their world. Know the shows they watch, the characters they like, their favorite ice cream, and favorite toys. Our staff subscribes to Nick Jr. and Disney and Me magazines to stay current with what preschoolers like.

- use down-to-earth words. Preschoolers are concrete thinkers; use words they can grasp concretely.

Small talk reaps big rewards. Take time to genuinely talk with the preschoolers in your ministry. They'll begin to smile and run to you when they see you coming. Then you'll see their hearts open to receive the biblical truths you want to impart to them.

—**Dale**

Daniel Has Left the Building

We've all had them—the children who thrive on being disruptive, the world-class escape artist, and the one your leaders say they can't handle. What do you do? Every child deserves a place in your preschool ministry, and it's your job to make sure you find the right combination of teacher and environment to make this happen.

There are many children who don't fit into the "cookie cutter" molds that our preschool ministries are developed around. Not every child will sit perfectly still on the designated carpet square in the middle of the room and listen to an adult tell a Bible story. Every child is unique and learns in different ways. No doubt when a child comes into your room, he or she comes with a reputation. As a leader you need to resist making prejudgments...and you don't even need to make a plan.

Be flexible. Flexibility is the secret. Maybe you have a child who's known to run out of the room; be flexible and wear flats instead of high heels. (I promise flats will increase your 100-yard-dash time.) Maybe you have a child who interrupts Bible time. Isn't life full of interruptions? Don't ignore the child; acknowledge him or her, and redirect everyone's attention back to the Bible.

Ignore labels. At a time when I had a group of 3-year-olds who were learning about Moses, a child came into my preschool ministry wearing an invisible label of "problem child." He was known to run, interrupt, not sit still, and not participate. When you hear this about a child, it's hard not to be apprehensive. But the experience I had with him forever changed me for the better.

This child was extremely intelligent and very much in his own world. Each week during the time before our devotional, he'd build an "office" in the corner of the room, and his office is where he'd insist on staying. For weeks I fought him on the office, telling him he had to take it down and come to the devotional with everyone else. During these first weeks, he'd always run out of the room.

Step out of the box. Then one week I stopped fighting and played along with this imaginary world he'd constructed for himself. Staying in character, we referred to our devotional as a lunch break from the office. In the following weeks sometimes this would work, and sometimes he'd stay in the office as I watched him from the doorway.

But once I'd stepped out of my traditional teacher mold and started being flexible and open to what he was doing, he stopped running and gradually began to participate. He'd stay in his office during Bible time but occasionally come out to teach the other preschoolers a song or bring me a plastic banana (his "phone") and tell me I had a call. I could see from these changes that he was letting us into his world, which was so much easier than us trying to force him into ours. I saw how open he was to sharing his world—while we had only wanted him in our world if he behaved and acted a certain way.

This child taught me a lot about God's love and understanding. And in one conference call on the plastic banana, guess who was on the other end—Moses!

—**Barbara**

'I'm in Training'

One of my family's all-time favorite TV shows is *Biggest Loser*. There's something compelling about seeing someone make a total transformation. We live for the final reveal. That's when all the blood, sweat, and tears pay off. Undeniably, the contestants with the best results are those who put forth the greatest effort. It's all in the training, baby.

I often tell parents that parenting preschoolers is simply a three- to four-year training camp. Sometimes it's not fun. It requires a lot of hard work; you must press forward even when you don't feel like it; consistency is a must—and there are times when you absolutely, positively want to quit. Put like this, it sounds almost impossible, doesn't it? Bottom line, parenting is hard work. But we trust the hard work to pay off at the final reveal.

Smack dab in the middle of the preschool training years comes the dreaded potty training, and parents need our support. Sunday isn't the time to tell parents, "Sorry, that's not our job." It *is* the time, however, to say, "We're here to help you, and together we can do this." Here are a few suggestions that will have your parents saying, "What a great preschool ministry!"

- **"I'm in Training" stickers**—Place stickers on the kids who are in training. Preschool ministry can get busy, and stickers help volunteers know which preschoolers are in training so they can reinforce this training while kids are at church.

- **"Parent communication" stickers**—Give preschoolers who go in the potty stickers that say, "I went in the potty," not as rewards but rather as a way to let parents know.

- **Offer training classes for parents.** Resource parents with information to help them be successful in this endeavor.

Remember, we're here to serve families, and this added touch to your ministry will have your young families feeling like VIPs.

—Gina

Digitykes

Today's preschoolers are growing up in a digital world. They'll never know life without computers, fast-advancing technology, cell phones, 24/7 connectedness, and nonstop media immersion. These children will be very different from previous generations with respect to technology.

Welcome to the digi-saturated world of the preschoolers in your ministry...

78% of preschool families own a computer.

69% of preschool families have Internet access.

7% of preschoolers have a computer in their bedroom.

26% of 4- to 6-year-olds use a computer on a typical day.

43% of 2- to 6-year-olds use a computer several times a week.

99.5% of preschool families have a TV.

75% of preschoolers watch television on a typical day.

43% of 3- and 4-year-olds have a TV in their bedroom.

51% of preschoolers with a television in their bedroom have connection to cable or satellite programming.

32% of preschoolers watch a DVD on a typical day.

18% of preschoolers have a television or DVD player in the car.

The development of handheld video game players for preschoolers is a multi-million dollar industry.

Children ages 4 to 6 spend almost two hours a day with media and technology.

74% of preschoolers know how to turn on the TV by themselves; 58% know how to use the remote to change channels by themselves; and 19% know how to turn on a computer by themselves.

Why are parents bringing their children up as "digikids" living media-centric lives?

- **For many families, it's a way of life.** Media has become part of the fabric of families' daily lives. Many families turn on the TV and leave it on even when no one is watching it. In any given day, 53 percent of children eat a snack or meals in front of the TV.

- **Parents believe media is key to their children's future success.** Many parents think their children need to get familiar with computers as early as possible.

   One mom from Columbus, Ohio, says, "They'll survive without the video games and TV...I don't think they'll survive without the computer. When they're older, they aren't going to have a cashier to check them out at Kroger."

- **Parents see it as an educational tool.** Research does show that educational programs such as *Sesame Street* can help preschoolers learn to read and count. Twenty million parents currently use the educational website jumpstart.com, which teaches children reading, math, and critical thinking skills.

   A mother of a preschooler in Irvine, California, says, "I don't spend nearly as much time with my son as I need to. He's learned huge amounts through the video and computer games that we have...I'm very grateful for the computer games. My kid learned his colors and letters from the computer. It's been very beneficial to us."

- **Parents use it to help with parenting.** Today's parents have a tough job. Often husbands and wives work and juggle complex schedules, and there are growing numbers of single parents. In this environment, parents often turn to media and technology as tools to help them manage their households and keep their children entertained while parents cook, do household chores, or enjoy some "me" time.

The debate rages among parents and educators as to whether and how technology, such as computers, should be used with young children. Some believe that bringing children into too many aspects of the adult world too soon is collapsing the stages of childhood. There are positive and negative points on both sides of the debate. No matter which side of the debate you land on, this much we know for sure: The preschoolers in our ministries are being raised in a digital, high-tech world. We must know how to minister to them effectively.

When ministering to digikids remember...

- **Nothing can replace caring volunteers who build relationships with preschoolers.** Technology and computers aren't a substitute for personal interaction. Research at 14 universities found that intelligence, academic success, and emotional stability were determined primarily by personal and language interaction with adults. Barbara Bowman of the Erikson Institute in Chicago says, "Even in the age of technology, it is through relationships with others—through joint activities, language, and shared feelings with other human beings—that children grasp meaning."

- **Honor their shorter attention spans.** Digitykes are used to rapid scene changes and quick edits. Researchers say that distracting graphics and special effects encourage stimulus-bound behavior that can contribute to shorter attention spans. This can cause reality to seem underwhelming or even boring in comparison. Break up preschool ministry time and learning into short, engaging, interactive segments.

- **Speak their language by using media and technology as a teaching method.** Technology and media can be great tools to share God's truth with digikids. Balance is the key. Video lessons every single week can become ineffective. Mix it up, using media and technology some weeks and live learning experiences on others.

- **Use media and technology to connect with today's digital parents.** Use the Internet, email, Twitter, and other methods to connect with parents and give them tools to disciple their children.

Childhood may have changed, but children haven't. Their hearts are still longing to know the God who made them and loves them. The message is still the same...even in a digital format.

—**Dale**

13

There's a Reason

I was once called to one of our preschool rooms because a little boy was having major behavioral issues—to the point where he kept running out of the room. I took him into the office and talked with him. When I asked about his father, his head dropped and he said, "I don't have a dad anymore...he's in jail."

I waited with him until his mom came to pick him up. After describing his behavior issues that day, I asked her about any major stress going on in his life. "Major stress" turned out to be an understatement. That week the father had come home and gotten extremely angry with the mother. When she fell asleep, he poured lighter fluid on her and tried to light her on fire. When that didn't work, he picked her up and slammed her down on the glass coffee table. He then picked up a piece of the broken glass and tried to slit her throat. She showed me several cuts on her arms. It had all happened in front of this little boy. The teenage sister was able to pull the father off the mother, and the police came. The father's in jail awaiting trial for attempted murder.

My heart broke for this child. No wonder he was having behavioral issues! Obviously he was experiencing a lot of fear and anxiety because of what he'd been through that week. This is an example of a child misbehaving at church when he or she has deeper issues going on. Many times when children go through troubled times in their lives or homes, feelings of anger, fear, or anxiety will surface at church. How do you minister to children when symptoms begin appearing that point toward deeper issues?

Connect with the parent immediately. Find out what's going on. Ask how you can meet the child's needs and minister to him or her during this time. Also offer help to the parents, and connect them with people who can meet their needs.

Give the child individual attention. This is when children need you the most. Many times misbehavior is a desperate cry for help. Be there for this child. Show unconditional love, support, and care. Meet with the child for a few minutes each week with the parent's permission. Connect the parent with a professional child counselor if needed. Assign a volunteer to be with the child one-on-one during class.

Request the parent's presence. If the misbehavior continues, ask the parent to stay with you in the room until the child's behavior improves. This may take several weeks.

The little boy I mentioned is doing much better. He's experienced a lot of pain for a child so young. But he's beginning to smile, and his behavior in class has improved dramatically. I know God has great plans for his life and will help this child rise above his painful memories.

Remember, there's always a reason children misbehave. If we can reach out in love to address the reason, we can see God do great work in their lives. He can bring healing, peace, and purpose to their hearts.

—**Dale**

14

Peer Pressure

We tend to think of peer pressure as something that occurs in the teen years. Actually, the influence of peers begins to take shape around the ages of 3 and 4. Like all human beings, preschoolers have a natural desire to fit in—to feel they're part of the group. As children interact more and more with other kids in preschool, they begin to feel pressure to conform to the group of peers they socialize with. This peer pressure influences how kids dress, the toys they play with, and the behaviors they engage in. Preschoolers will go out of their way to think and act like their friends—in positive and negative ways.

Along with their parents, we provide preschoolers with building blocks of faith and give them values that guide them. But our ministries are uniquely positioned to increase the power of positive peer pressure in three distinct ways.

1. We help preschoolers know they're not alone. When it comes to standing up to the negative influences of their peers, preschoolers need to know that other children their age are also learning and believing the same things about God and living their lives according to God's Word. They'll engage in Bible learning, worship, and crafts with their peers at church because they enjoy being part of the group.

2. We show preschoolers how to apply God's Word. Children become what we show them, not what we tell them. By using real-life scenarios, we can show preschoolers how to live out the Bible's teachings. By incorporating puppets, videos, and drama sketches into our preschool lessons, we can show kids examples of how they can make Christlike choices and overcome negative social influences.

3. We acknowledge preschoolers who lead by example. Children will repeat what gets rewarded. When you see an example of positive peer pressure in action, go out of your way to identify and applaud the child for influencing his or her peers in a positive way. Be alert and ready to praise when you see a child engage in worship, participate in ministry experiences, and listen intently during Bible time.

The influence preschoolers have on their friends can be helpful or harmful. Through our ministry's positive influence, children can be strengthened to resist negative peer pressure when they're outside our doors.

—Eric

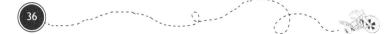

The Angry Child

Anger is part of life—everyone gets angry. But helping angry preschoolers presents a unique challenge because anger is their response to feelings they don't know how to cope with or verbalize. These could be frustration, fear, jealousy, embarrassment, or even boredom.

The best thing we can do in a preschool ministry setting is to try to prevent situations that can cause anger. But when we find ourselves with a child who's angry, we must be ready to recognize the underlying problem and find a solution to prevent the anger from continuing, escalating, or spreading to other children. Here are typical causes for a preschooler's anger.

Boredom—Too often we want to diagnose a child with a problem when he or she acts out aggressively or with anger. Could it be that the child just isn't receiving the right amount of stimulation? If you don't suspect a serious underlying problem, consider that the child may simply be bored. Anger management for young children often means helping them to focus their energy in other, more creative ways. A preschool ministry that has too few activities and restricts movement can lead to boredom that manifests itself through anger in some children.

If a child is refusing to participate in activities or being destructive with items around them or intentionally being a distraction to other children, he or she probably needs more physical and creative outlets. Reconsider your ministry environment, and see how time could be restructured to utilize more movement and creative storytelling. Provide a variety of outlets so children can refocus their energy.

Frustration—Frustration is a tense, unhappy feeling that often results from being unable to do something we want to do. An adult will walk away from this kind of situation, ask for help, and then try again. But a preschool child is unable to recognize the frustration and what's causing it, so the feeling will quickly turn into anger, usually directed at the task.

To prevent frustration anger, keep your preschool ministry experiences at the correct developmental stage for all the children. Understand that crafts requiring fine motor skills, writing, and even coloring can create a separation of abilities among children. Carefully plan your experiences in a way that ensures no child is left behind. Also, remember to give ample encouragement to all children for even the smallest accomplishments.

Jealousy—The green-eyed monster is a common problem with children. Jealousy can rear its head at a very early age in preschoolers because of an inward need to be recognized for who they are. It's often triggered by sibling rivalry if a sibling has more privileges, attention, or freedom. Peer pressure can become a huge factor in jealousy if a child doesn't have the same material things friends have. This can cause a child to feel left out, mistreated, or that life is "unfair."

To prevent jealousy in your preschool ministry, avoid comparisons. Even something as simple as holding up a child's paper because you think it's exceptional can stir up feelings of jealousy and make another child angry. Preschool children also have difficulty when they think someone else receives special attention from an adult. What they may see as inequality in attention can cause jealousy toward the other child. Be very intentional about treating each child with equal love and praise.

Embarrassment—As ministry leaders, we know how wrong it is to draw negative attention to a child; for example, reprimanding a child for not paying attention, laughing at something he or she did, or even calling the child by a nickname. When discipline is necessary and could embarrass a child, do it as privately as possible or address the issue after preschool ministry is over.

Fear—This emotion usually comes from a home atmosphere in which a child loses his or her sense of well-being. Maybe the parental relationship isn't good, a child is involved in a custody battle, or the child has a new sibling and fears the loss of love.

To deal with children's anger in this situation, it's important to understand their fear. Ask them what they're feeling, what's happened, or what's gone wrong. They may or may not be able to tell you clearly, but all of us, especially children, are remarkably able to heal when given the support we need.

Reassurance and comfort can come in many forms. Verbal and nonverbal communication is essential. Remind preschoolers verbally that they're loved and cared for, and nonverbally offer your physical support by hugging them or just sitting down together.

—**Barbara**

16
Doers of the Word

"But don't just listen to God's Word. You must do what it says."

—(James 1:22)

Preschoolers learn best by doing. Studies show that we retain very little of what we hear but a high percentage of what we do. Preschoolers are *wired* to *do*. Sitting quietly for more than a few minutes...it's not happening.

Here's how we can help children learn by being doers of the Word.

Have them "do" the Bible, not just listen to it. Get them involved in acting out the Scripture for the day; let everyone have a part.

Send home "do-votionals," not just devotionals. Give kids activities they can do at home with their parents to reinforce and help them live out the truth they're learning in your preschool ministry.

Use hands-on, active, experiential learning. Trade in the lecture for learning by doing. Preschoolers love learning by touching, constructing, and creating. Recently I was teaching the weekend lesson for our preschoolers. The lesson truth was "We are the church." I gathered all the children around me and gave each of them a building block. We then proceeded to build a church building. Each child added his or her block to the building, and I must say it was a magnificent piece of architecture. Which means it didn't fall down!

After we were all done, I asked the children where the church was. They pointed to the little church building we'd constructed. Then I told them that the church isn't a building...it's people...it's us. I asked them to touch someone beside them and say, "We are the church." As they did this, they got it.

It was awesome to see them understand that the church wasn't made of blocks. It was made of them, children Jesus loves.

Let's continue building the faith of preschoolers by teaching them to be doers of the Word and not just hearers.

—**Dale**

17

They Know My Name

I'll never forget pulling into the parking lot of my freshman college dorm for the first time, excited and scared to death. As I got out of the car, I thought to myself, *What in the world do I do now?* Just then I heard a voice calling out, "Gina Jackson, I'm so glad you're here." It was my dorm mom, Melanie. When I heard my name, the butterflies left and my heart filled with peace and great expectation. Melanie made a connection with me that day that we kept throughout my college years. How would my circumstances have been different if no one had noticed me when I arrived? I know for certain it would've changed a lot of things.

When someone speaks our name, an instant connection is made. You and your volunteer staff will set yourselves apart as leaders by how well you remember names.

Sundays are about connecting with preschoolers and connecting with their parents. It's vitally important to learn the names of the families who enter your church facilities each week. Great leaders will spend time on this. It's a discipline and a habit you must work on to master.

- **Take photos.** The best way to learn the names of your preschoolers is to take their pictures—but ask parents' permission first, and have them sign release forms.

- **Make information cards.** After you print each child's photo, cut it out and attach it to a 4x6-inch card. Write the child's name, parents' names, and any other information you'd like. You can make this fun by asking preschoolers to tell you their favorite foods, colors, sports, songs, or TV shows. Review these cards to help you not only remember their names but also to learn more about them.

Making an all-out effort to learn every child's name is a true act of love and a confirmation of your commitment to preschoolers and their families.

—Gina

Let's Play!

I remember having time to play when I was a child. Every minute of my day wasn't scheduled. I was allowed to have fun by using my imagination.

Fast-forward to today. Busy families are working harder than ever. American fathers work an average of 51 hours a week, and mothers work 41 hours a week on average. So parents try to maximize their time with their children by creating the "organized kid." It seems every moment of a child's day is scheduled. Children today have 12 hours less free time each week than kids did in 1981. Forty percent of school districts in America have eliminated recess. Dr. Jack Wetter, director of UCLA's department of pediatric psychology, says, "I see small children so programmed they have no leisure time." Many parents today have gotten caught up in the false belief that free play is unimportant or even a waste of time. We've turned children into miniature adults.

But studies have shown that play is vitally important in a child's life. Children need free time to explore, use their imaginations, and just be kids. Play is also a learning opportunity in disguise. Play promotes development, problem solving, and creativity. It helps build better attention spans and encourages social development.

Is play an element of your preschool ministry? Are you giving children the opportunity to develop and learn through play? If we asked preschoolers in your ministry whether they get to play at church, what would they say?

An effective ministry creates a fun and playful environment for preschoolers. Preschoolers aren't miniature adults. They're children. They need to laugh, giggle, play, and have fun. One of the most important things you can do is make your preschool ministry fun.

Allow preschoolers free time to play at church. Set up play centers that children can experience before your preschool ministry begins. Let them have time to be spontaneous. Give them time to just goof off.

Build a team of preschool volunteers who like to have fun and play. The attitude and demeanor of your volunteer leaders will determine the atmosphere of your preschool environment. Find people who are gifted to be in preschool ministry. You'll recognize them by their spirit of fun—they like to play with kids! Research has proven that the level of children's play rises when adults play with them.

Use play as a teaching tool. Knowing facts alone isn't enough. Just because a preschooler can repeat something doesn't mean he or she has learned it. Everyone learns from meaningful experiences. Play that's hands-on, interactive, and focused promotes learning that lasts. Companies such as LeapFrog have discovered this and are producing toys that teach. Offer guided play opportunities in your preschool ministry that teach kids God's Word. Group's Hands-On Bible Curriculum® (group.com) provides toys and other objects to use as teaching tools.

Play is to early childhood what gas is to a car. May our preschool hallways be filled with the sounds of kids playing instead of "shhh." May our preschool rooms be filled with smiling faces that come from playful activities instead of frowns from being made to sit still. Having fun is key to a thriving preschool ministry. Let's play!

—**Dale**

Hello, God

Teaching preschoolers how to pray can be challenging, and using rote memorization or words a child wouldn't normally use won't develop an understanding of the true meaning of prayer. We need to emphasize simple prayers that come from the heart and help preschoolers build a relationship with God through conversation.

Follow these simple guidelines to help preschoolers talk to God.

Emphasize that we're talking to God and that God loves and cares for us. God, as an unseen being, is a difficult concept for children to understand, so keep your explanation of God very simple.

Use plain language. When we use language that's formal or unfamiliar, we communicate the idea that God is formal and unreachable.

Don't insist on a specific body position. While closing our eyes may help us concentrate, preschoolers can become distracted by the challenge of keeping their eyes closed.

Encourage preschoolers to give thanks for things that are important in their lives. Giving thanks for their parents, pets, food, and friends will make sense to their level of understanding. Never tell a child that what he or she is praying for is wrong. At this stage preschoolers are developing a relationship with God as a friend and confidant.

Don't ask a preschooler to pray in front of others unless you know he or she is comfortable doing so. It's better to ask if someone wants to volunteer to pray.

Help preschoolers understand that prayer is a way of asking for help for themselves or others. As they learn to express their hearts and concerns through prayer, children will build trust in God and a foundation of faith.

Use creative experiences to help preschoolers pray. Preschoolers are visual learners, and teaching prayer in an abstract manner makes it harder for them to understand. Instead have them each create a prayer book, a prayer box, or similar item. Then encourage them to draw, color, or bring pictures of things they'd like to include in their prayers. Have them each keep their "prayers" in their book or box and add other prayers over time. This simple concept will help them move into the next stage of their prayer lives as they grow in age and understanding.

—**Barbara**

Preschoolers are learners. They constantly perceive and discover new ways of doing things. Research has shown that children this age are especially receptive to learning; their brains are like sponges picking up concepts through the use of all their senses.

One of the best things our preschool ministries can do is to offer children experiences that help them truly learn God's Word. The beauty of teaching young children to soak in God's Word is that they haven't developed preconceived notions about the truth in the Bible.

Our preschool ministries should be primed and ready to help these natural learners learn. The good news is that kids learn best with people they love and when learning is fun. This means that when kids develop relationships with ministry volunteers and have fun experiences—they're in their tailor-made learning environment. Use these key elements to help preschoolers learn.

Relationships—At our church, we create a setting that's conducive for preschoolers to soak up God's Word by having consistent volunteers in our preschool ministry. Preschoolers can't build a meaningful relationship with a volunteer who only serves once a month. While we strongly encourage all our preschool volunteers to serve on a weekly basis, we require that they serve at least twice a month to maintain consistency for our preschoolers. We've found this still allows relationships to be formed between our volunteers and our kids. These loving relationships provide a favorable environment where preschoolers can learn and soak up God's Word.

Fun Experiences—We do everything we can to make the Bible come alive for our kids by incorporating games, hands-on activities, and creativity. The last thing we want a preschooler to say as he or she leaves our church is "It was boring," and we do everything in our power to keep that from happening.

I was in the lobby recently saying goodbye to families as they left, and I noticed a 3-year-old who was crying. When I asked the parents what had happened, they said it was their first time to visit our church, and their child didn't want to leave. They've been attending ever since. This should be our goal every week—kids having such a good time soaking in God's Word that they don't want to leave when their parents come to pick them up.

—**Eric**

What's Going On in There?

Were you aware that at birth our brains have almost all the neurons they will ever have? The brain continues to grow after birth, but it reaches 95 percent of its adult size by the age of 4. A look at the incredible milestones occurring during the preschool years of life gives a whole new perspective on what to expect from these little ones with brains almost as big as ours.

Here's some of the amazing progress preschoolers make each year.

3 Years—Children in this age group love to talk and sing. They're able to answer simple questions such as "What are you doing?" "What is this?" and "Where?" They also *ask* a lot of questions—oftentimes just to keep the conversation going. By 3, a child will use sentences of three or more words and have a vocabulary of 300 to 1,000 words. Children begin to describe what they're seeing and doing and start using words to reason things out. Three-year-olds can hold crayons between their first two fingers and thumb, use blunt scissors, stack nine or 10 blocks, wash and dry their hands, and catch a large bounced ball with their arms. They like to look at books and will listen attentively to age-appropriate stories. They can copy a rough circle or cross, and they can work puzzles with large pieces.

4 Years—At this age children have a growing understanding of past, present, and future, and they're able to follow familiar routines on their own. Typically, 4-year-olds have a vocabulary of 1,000 words and use sentences of up to eight words. They can answer the questions "Whose?" "Who" "Why?" and "How many?" They jump well, run fast, hop on one foot, and climb ladders, trees, and playground equipment. Children this age enjoy sorting objects into groups; they can form shapes and objects with clay, such as snakes, cookies, and simple animals, and build block structures that are vertical and horizontal. They like stories about how things grow and how things operate. They're able to hold a crayon using a tripod grasp and reproduce some shapes and letters. Four-year-olds paint and draw with purpose, but when they have trouble implementing the ideas they have in mind, they may call their creations something else.

5 Years—Five-year-olds know thousands of words and can say them clearly. They can describe people and events in detail and use complex sentences. At this age, children understand and use time concepts such as yesterday, tomorrow, day, and night. They ask innumerable questions such as "Why?" "What?" "Where?" and "How?" This is a stage where children make great strides physically. Five-year-olds are in constant motion and can't sit still. They can skip using alternate feet, walk backward, jump or hop forward 10 times in a row, and balance on either foot. They can catch a ball from three feet away and ride a tricycle with speed and skill. They can count to 20 or more and identify four to eight colors. Many children at this age know the alphabet and can reproduce lots of shapes and letters. Most 5-year-olds demonstrate fair control of a pencil or marker, and are able to cut on the line with scissors (although not perfectly).

—**Barbara**

Special Delivery

A few years ago, while she was in high school, Mary Grace asked me if she could teach preschoolers. I was thrilled because 13 years prior she'd been one of *my* preschoolers. It doesn't get any better than that.

One Sunday afternoon after Mary Grace had been with us awhile, I invited my leaders to come together to share their prayer requests, celebrate victories, and unload their burdens. During this meeting as we discussed our preschoolers, some leaders shared heartwarming stories of things their preschoolers had said; others told about special moments when they'd seen in preschoolers' eyes that true learning had taken place.

A little message of love can go a long way. In the middle of the meeting, Mary Grace asked if she could share something with us. She told us that when she was in preschool, many of the preschool leaders would send her cards each week. Some would say, "I'm praying for you"; others might say, "I'm glad you were here." She told us she couldn't wait to check the mail each day. It was the highlight of her week. She said she'd kept every card in a box in her room, and she still had them today. Here was a young, beautiful, Christlike woman, who was blessed to have others pour their lives into hers and is still reaping the benefits today.

Her story had a great impact on all those who were in that meeting. It was a gentle but powerful reminder of how small acts can have a lifelong effect. Snail mail still works—and preschoolers love it.

Mr. Postman, look and see. I send out birthday cards to every preschooler on his or her birthday. I've had moms tell me their children will carry those birthday cards around until they literally fall apart. These simple little cards make them feel special, loved, and valued.

Encourage your leaders to write to their preschoolers on a regular basis. Help them find success in this by providing cards, labels, postage, and a mail drop. This small effort will bring lots of smiles to preschoolers.

—Gina

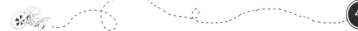

Over and Over Again

As adults we know that learning through repetition is an aspect of studying most people dread. But studies show that by the second day after we've learned something, we've forgotten 50 percent. By day 30, we retain 2 to 3 percent of the knowledge, and if there's no review, we won't retain the information at all after a month. Repetition as an instrument of education is how we learn as adults and children.

Why preschoolers need repetition—By repeating words and phrases, you're reinforcing neural pathways that link sound and meaning in preschoolers' brains. Hearing something over and over again helps preschoolers remember information for increasing periods of time. Repetition allows children to build on what they've learned. Preschoolers need repetition of biblical truth to help them gain knowledge and confidence in the Bible.

Why preschoolers love repetition—Once children have learned something, they enjoy repetition because they know what comes next. Children love the predictability that comes from hearing the same Bible passage or song over and over again. Repetition makes children feel more secure and in control because they feel they can predict what's going to happen.

In our preschool ministries, keeping to a strict routine helps children relax. Ask preschoolers, "What will we do next?" and they'll be able to tell you exactly what activity they're expecting. And if you don't follow the routine, they'll quickly point out your mistake.

Incorporating repetition into our ministries is essential for preschoolers. For younger preschoolers, this means the same routine can continue for a year, with activities varying as children increase in age. By the time children approach kindergarten age, they're able to accept change in routine every three months. Follow this principle, and you'll have attentive learners and eager participants.

—**Barbara**

Preschool Ministry

Get a Clue From Blue's Clues

Blue's Clues, a children's TV show that aired on Nickelodeon from 1996 until 2006, was one of the most successful, critically acclaimed, and groundbreaking preschool shows of all time. The main character was an animated dog named Blue, and the show's host was a guy named Steve. Malcolm Gladwell, in his book *The Tipping Point,* called the show "perhaps the stickiest TV show ever." By sticky, he means irresistible and involving.

Within 18 months of its premiere, virtually 100 percent of preschoolers' parents in America knew about *Blue's Clues*. More than 10 million *Blue's Clues* books were in print by 2001, and more than 3 million copies of CD titles had been sold. By 2002, 13.7 million viewers tuned in each week.

Preschool ministries can learn a lot from *Blue's Clues*...

Reach preschoolers through stories. Children's educational shows before *Blue's Clues* used a magazine format made up of a variety of segments. *Blue's Clues* changed all that by telling a single story from beginning to end in each episode. Left-to-right camera movement and scene transitions had the rhythm and motion of pages turning in a child's storybook.

- Use stories to communicate truth.

- Present each story in an engaging and exciting way. The *way* you tell the story is important.

Use preschooler's everyday activities and places as the background for your teaching. The settings and scenes for *Blue's Clues* reflected children's everyday lives.

- Use places and things that are familiar to children.

- Use everyday objects as teaching tools. Jesus did this when he taught; he used birds, flowers, coins, gates, and sheep.

- Keep it simple and age-appropriate.

Focus on active participation instead of passive viewing. The premise behind *Blue's Clues* was to have children intellectually and behaviorally active during the show. Up until the time the show was created, children's educational TV had presented content in a one-way conversation. But *Blue's Clues* addressed questions directly to the children watching and paused to let kids think and respond. The creators believed that if children were more involved in the action of what they viewed, they'd stay engaged longer. They were right!

- Use active learning. Get kids actively involved in every part of your preschool ministry, including the teaching time.
- Ask lots of questions. Give children time to respond.
- Remember kids learn more by doing than by listening.

Kid-test your programming. Every episode was field-tested three times before it aired. Producers had groups of preschool children watch the show. They made notes when children looked away, which meant kids were disengaged. Then producers went back and adjusted those parts of the show to make them more engaging.

- Look through the eyes of a preschooler when planning. Make sure elements are age-appropriate.
- During your preschool ministry, watch for times when children become restless or start looking around. Modify these segments to be more interactive and compelling.

Emphasize repetition to ensure retention. The same episode of *Blue's Clues* aired daily for five days before the next one aired. Children's attention and comprehension increased with each repeated viewing. Repetition was also built into each episode. For example, in one episode the host says some variation of the word *predict* 15 times.

- Less is more. Decide what basic, must-know truths you want preschoolers to learn, and focus on those truths.
- Repeat the main lesson point multiple times each week.

Get the right people on your team. Producers carefully chose characters and voices for the show. After months of research they picked out the host, Steve Burns, from more than 100 people who auditioned. They cast Tracie Paige Johnson as Blue's voice because she sounded the most like a dog.

- Don't just focus on filling positions—find people who are gifted and called to the roles in your preschool ministry.

Engage children in problem solving. Steve, the host, presented the audience with a puzzle that involved Blue. The audience then worked through a series of games that were mini-puzzles related to the overall puzzle. At the end of the show, the clues came together to uncover the answer.

- Challenge preschoolers to think. Move beyond simple yes and no questions. Pose questions that'll spark dialogue.

- Guide children to *discover* answers instead of being *told* answers.

Rent or buy a set of *Blue's Clues* DVDs and look for more clues on how to effectively communicate to preschoolers.

—**Dale**

Play-Schoolers

Preschoolers have a natural propensity to play. Not only is play natural for them, it's also essential for their overall development. Through play, children discover how to express themselves and interact socially. Play also helps young children explore and understand their world. Play facilitates learning for preschoolers. While play is essential to the physical, emotional, and social development of children, it's key to their spiritual development as well. Here are four practical ways to incorporate play into your preschool programming.

1. Use make-believe. For preschoolers, the opportunity to pretend gives them the ability to comprehend. Pretending expands children's life experiences by letting them be whoever they desire to be. Through pretending, children can investigate and appreciate the world around them. Pretend play opens up preschoolers' imaginations and allows them to express themselves creatively. Use arts and crafts in your preschool programming, and incorporate pretend play by letting kids dress up and role-play the Bible.

2. Make it learner-based. Our lessons must be learner-based to effectively reach preschoolers. In a Children's Ministry Magazine article, "What's the Matter With Christian Education?" author Thom Schultz shares four techniques that Jesus used to help people genuinely learn:

- **Start with the preschoolers' context.** Look for ways to connect the Bible to something that's familiar to preschoolers, and keep in mind that play is their natural learning context.

- **Allow preschoolers to discover truth.** Ask open-ended questions that help children discover the truth on their own.

- **Take advantage of teachable moments.** Teachable moments occur throughout your preschool ministry time. Notice when your kids are most attentive, and use these times to teach because kids are most ready to learn. This might mean coming alongside preschoolers as they play and modeling biblical truth for them; for example, how to treat others.

- **Provide preschoolers with opportunities to practice what they've learned.** Application is the glue that makes your lessons stick. Create fun experiences that help preschoolers apply what they're learning.

3. Keep kids active. Kids shouldn't be sitting in circle time or at tables during most of preschool ministry; they should be moving. So push back those chairs, and keep your kids on the go. Keep them active in worship—don't just have them repeat a Scripture verse; come up with motions. Active games are another great way to help preschoolers learn. The truth is they're going to move anyway, so you might as well incorporate it into your programming.

4. Stimulate the senses—Provide preschoolers with learning centers where they can hear, see, touch, smell, or taste an element connected to what they're learning. For example, if you're teaching about Creation, take preschoolers outside, and let them see, hear, and touch what God has made. Let them smell frankincense at Christmas. Let them taste unleavened bread when you teach them about the Passover or Lord's Supper.

Incorporating these principles of play into your preschool programming will make better teachers. Your preschool ministry will be more fun; the kids will learn and have a blast doing it. And you'll enjoy coming up with new and creative ways to play.

—**Eric**

I'm Going to Be a Big Kid!

Every preschooler wants to be a big kid. Three-year-olds want to be 4-year-olds. Four-year-olds want to be 5-year-olds. Kindergartners want to be in first grade with the big kids. In just a blink of time, the preschoolers in your ministry will transition into elementary ministry. Parents get anxious as they see their "babies" getting older; some preschoolers are fearful about moving into a new environment. It's important to have a strategic action plan to help your preschoolers become big kids.

1. Start at least two months before the transition with "transition touches." The more you can acclimate your preschoolers beforehand, the less anxious they'll be. For example:

- **Eight weeks out**—Have someone from the elementary team visit the kindergartners, introduce him- or herself, and tell kids about the upcoming transition.

- **Six weeks out**—Have the elementary team member visit the kindergartners again to build excitement about the upcoming transition.

- **Four weeks out**—Have the elementary team member visit the kindergartners and lead a small part of your preschool ministry session.

- **Two weeks out**—Have the elementary team member visit the kindergartners and lead the entire session.

- **One week out**—Take your kindergartners over to the elementary ministry for part of the session.

2. Communicate with parents about their children's transition. Inform parents well in advance about the upcoming transition. Invite them to an open house in their children's new ministry environment.

3. Have a graduation ceremony for kindergartners who are transitioning up. It's great if you can incorporate this into an adult service. Present kids with a gift, such as a Bible. This is also a great opportunity to speak into the lives of parents and encourage them to lead their children spiritually.

4. Work closely with the elementary team to help children transition smoothly. In many churches there's disconnection between the preschool and elementary ministries. Develop a close partnership, and work as one team to build children's faith foundation. This partnership can be especially beneficial when it's time for kids to transition.

If kindergartners are included in your elementary ministry, you can follow this same plan with the preschoolers who are transitioning into kindergarten.

God is at work in preschoolers' lives. As they become big kids, let's ask God to give them a big faith foundation.

—**Dale**

27

Special Events: Not Just VBS

Churches usually overlook preschool ministries when it comes to special events. But this omission represents an immeasurable loss of opportunity to develop relationships and outreach into the community. Families with preschool children often feel isolated and alone—they need opportunities to connect to a church and develop Christian friendships. Special events can open the door.

The first thought that comes to mind when you think of hosting a new event is probably, *Where would I find more volunteers?* But you'll likely only need a few helpers because children won't be unaccompanied; they'll be with parents, grandparents, or other adults. This is also a perfect time to enlist the help of your church leaders so they can acquaint themselves with preschoolers and their families. Remember to keep everything simple, fun, and child-friendly. Set your sights on the following goals for these events:

1. Provide parents with inexpensive bonding time with their children.

2. Help young families in your church get to know each other.

3. Give parents a chance to invite neighbors with preschoolers to a non-threatening church event.

4. Give yourself and other leaders an opportunity to get to know the children and families in your ministry in an informal atmosphere.

When deciding on events for preschoolers, look for inspiration from Disney, holiday seasons, birthday parties, and popular games or cartoon characters. Create a theme and play it up. Many of these can be translated into Bible experiences—or just design them as fun experiences for preschoolers and parents.

Create events that can be repeated every year. Keep costs down by shopping garage sales and asking church members to donate items. If you don't have a budget for these events, charge each family a small fee to cover the cost of food—but be sure visiting families come free.

Below are several suggestions for special events, but the sky's the limit, and the only rule is to have fun!

Princess Tea—What little girl doesn't want to be a princess? This event includes having everyone dressed in their Sunday best, a photo opportunity, activities such as the girls getting their nails painted or faces glittered, and a special "princess" menu.

Western BBQ—Put on the country music ,and get out the lassos because the boys will love being cowboys for a night. A menu of barbeque, chips, and root beer is perfect to begin a night of roping the calf (a painted piñata) and playing Pin the Badge on the Sheriff and Tin Can Shoot Out.

Bible Times Dinner—This event is a simple dinner where preschoolers and families meet people from the Bible. Children each get an autograph book and an opportunity to meet the people they know about from the Bible, hear their stories, and have them sign their books. This is a great way to bring the Bible to life!

 Drive-In Movie Night—Show a movie on the side of your building for this summertime event, and have families bring lawn chairs or blankets. For extra fun, provide a few games for the families before the movie begins.

Kids Care—Create an event to help preschoolers learn to serve. They can do simple projects such as filling diaper bags for foster care programs, drawing pictures to send to those who are shut-in, or sacking groceries for a food pantry.

Special events for preschoolers are offered so rarely that you'll be over-whelmed with appreciation from families and quickly find that these fun times become permanent features of your ministry.

—**Barbara**

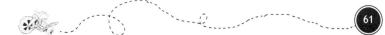

28

May I Have Your Attention, Please?

Growing up, my teachers and parents were constantly telling me to "pay attention" and "focus, focus, focus." Now that I'm an adult, I realize my problem wasn't the inability to pay attention—my problem was that I paid attention to everything!

I wasn't very different from the children in your preschool ministry. You probably find yourself struggling, as my teachers did, to get the kids in your preschool ministry to pay attention. The majority of the time it's not that they're ignoring you or being disobedient; they're just paying attention to everything around them. Preschoolers naturally have short attention spans and are easily distracted, so we need to implement some best practices to help them stay focused.

- **Change often.** To maintain kids' focus, you have to keep things moving. Don't spend too much time on any one thing. The majority of your preschoolers can only focus on one experience for three or four minutes, so if you're planning to spend 10 minutes on a Bible lesson...don't. Seriously, don't do it. If you do, you'll spend more time trying to keep kids' attention than you'll spend teaching them anything.

- **Plan More Than You Need.** You must be well-prepared if you want a chance at keeping your preschoolers' attention. This means you need to plan more than you can possibly use and move seamlessly from one game or experience to another. There's nothing worse than running out of things to do on a Sunday morning in preschool ministry. Staring into the eyes of those children, knowing that you've completed your lesson and you have eight minutes left to go before parents arrive can be daunting. So always have an extra game, a fun song, or a simple craft ready to go at a moment's notice.

—Eric

"The leading priests and the teachers of religious law saw these wonderful miracles and heard even the children in the Temple shouting, 'Praise God for the Son of David.' But the leaders were indignant. They asked Jesus, 'Do you hear what these children are saying?' 'Yes,' Jesus replied. 'Haven't you ever read the Scriptures? For they say, "You have taught children and infants to give you praise." ' "

—(Matthew 21:15-16)

Preschoolers can praise God! It's awesome watching them worship God in innocence and wonder. Here's how to lay the foundation for preschoolers to become lifetime worshippers.

- **Choose fun, energetic worship leaders.** People who have lots of smiles will set the atmosphere for the children. Middle school and high school kids make great worship leaders for preschoolers.

- **Use lively worship songs.** Many great songs are available on DVD. Some of our favorite praise DVDs are *Play-n-Worship* and *Shine!* (group.com), *Praise Party—My Best Friend* (yancynotnancy.com), and *Believin' On* (janaalayra.com).

- **Use the same songs frequently.** Preschoolers love to sing the same songs again and again. Pick at least one song each month to repeat every week so they can learn it. Introduce new songs as they learn current songs.

- **Give preschoolers opportunities to worship with their parents.** Once a quarter we have a worship experience for children and their parents. Part of the service involves the preschoolers coming up and singing worship songs. Parents love to see their children worshipping.

- **Make preschool worship songs available for parents to purchase.** Preschoolers enjoy singing worship songs with their parents in the car and at home, so purchase copies of the CDs and DVDs, and make them available to parents. When you partner with parents and they begin worshipping with their children during the week, you multiply the power of worship in preschoolers' lives.

- **Teach preschoolers the purpose of worship.** Let children know they're praising God when they worship. Teach them they're sending their love up to God when they sing to him. Take a few seconds to remind them of this truth each week as they prepare to sing.

—**Dale**

Characters Wanted

Preschoolers love characters. Just take a group of 4-year-olds to Chuck E. Cheese and watch their excitement. Trust me, they're not excited about the pizza...they're eager to dance and sing with the oversized mouse. And what's the #1 thing that children want to do at Walt Disney World? You guessed it— they want get up close to meet and greet the Disney characters. I think it's time for our preschool ministries to take a cue from these two preschooler hot spots and utilize over-the-top personalities and mascots to connect with our kids and teach them biblical truth. Here's why.

Characters connect with preschoolers. An over-the-top persona taps into children's innate curiosity and their desire to use their imaginations. Preschoolers can begin to see themselves in the characters. They want to be like the characters you have on stage.

Characters engage preschoolers' attention. Characters are a great way to grab kids' attention and *keep* their attention while you teach them biblical truth.

Characters make kids laugh. Kids identify with and learn from these characters because they make kids laugh. Characters create a buzz with the kids and families at your church that can spread throughout your community.

In our preschool ministry, we use various characters to get kids excited about coming to church. They help us meet preschoolers where they are and teach truth that's eternally significant. We have three main characters and a preschool mascot that engage kids, connect with them, and create a fun environment for learning about God. Meet our characters.

Mr. Manners—Mr. Manners dresses in a tuxedo and is very prim and proper. His primary role is to help us teach preschoolers how God wants us to treat others. Whenever we communicate something from the Bible that deals with our relationship with other people, Mr. Manners makes a guest appearance in our preschool ministry. He assists us in teaching our preschoolers to obey their parents, love their neighbors, and treat others the way they want to be treated.

Georgia Jones—From stories of David fighting Goliath to Joshua sending spies into Jericho, God's Word is full of adventure. Whenever the Bible lesson involves adventure, we use our character, Georgia Jones, to teach the lesson to our preschoolers. Georgia Jones is our version of...you guessed it...Indiana Jones. Complete with leather jacket and theme music, Georgia Jones teaches preschoolers that following God is never dull.

Fisherman Fred—Whether we're teaching about Moses parting the Red Sea, Jonah and the big fish, or any other Bible account that deals with water, Fisherman Fred is there to set the hook and grab our preschoolers' attention. He wears a camouflage hat, carries a huge fishing pole, and can tell a tale as only a fisherman can.

Kodiak the Bear—We not only use characters to teach the Bible, we also have a preschool mascot. Kodiak is an oversized bear that welcomes families as they arrive at our preschool department. There's nothing like watching the smile on preschoolers' faces and the joy in their eyes as they line up to high-five Kodiak on their way to their rooms.

Every week our cast of characters and our friendly mascot get kids excited about being at church.

—**Eric**

31

Praying for Your Preschoolers

"The Church has not yet touched the fringe of the possibilities of intercessory prayer."

—John Mott

The greatest thing we can do for the preschoolers in our ministry is pray for them. We say this and know it—but do we do it? Do we get so busy putting together crafts and disinfecting toys and running off coloring sheets and buying fish-shaped crackers and picking out worship songs and all the rest on an unending list...that we don't do the most important thing? It's time to move intercessory prayer for our preschoolers to the top of our priority list.

Recently we took a strategic step in this direction. We spent hours and hours seeking God for prayer verses that we could pray over the preschoolers in our ministry. Here are the prayer verses we chose from the Scripture God led us to:

"May the Lord bless you and protect you" (Numbers 6:24).

"May the Lord smile on you and be gracious to you" (Numbers 6:25).

"May the Lord show you his favor and give you his peace" (Numbers 6:26).

"May the Lord keep you from all harm and watch over your life...now and forever" (Psalm 121:7-8).

"May you experience the love of Christ, though it is too great to understand fully" (Ephesians 3:19).

"May you grow in the grace and knowledge of our Lord and Savior Jesus Christ" (2 Peter 3:18).

"For I know the plans I have for you," says the Lord. "They are plans for good...to give you a future and a hope" (Jeremiah 29:11).

Each preschool ministry room has one of these verses painted on the wall. Our preschool volunteers gather to pray for the children before they arrive. Then during class, they silently pray the verse over the children several times. As children grow and move through our preschool ministry rooms, they're interceded for hundreds of times with each of these verses.

It means so much to parents to know that their children are intentionally prayed for each week. We also partner with parents by giving them a copy of the verses so they pray them over their children at home. A prayer partnership between home and church makes an eternal difference in a preschooler's life.

The greatest thing you can do for your preschool ministry is make it a house of prayer!

—**Dale**

32

Did a Big Fish Really Swallow Jonah?

My greatest fear in life is waking up one day and finding a generation of young people who've completely walked away from the Christian faith. There's one thing that gets me out of bed every morning, and that's the fact that someone must get in there and fight for the hearts and minds of these children.

As preschool leaders, it's important for us to realize this truth. We have the ability to influence an entire generation. God has called us to diligently put his Word into their hearts. How can we as leaders teach our preschoolers the unchanging truth of God's Word?

Tell them again and again that what we tell them from the Bible is true. This means it really happened. In an ordinary day for preschoolers, more than likely they'll view media that's based on fantasy or fairy tales. That's okay. We don't need to get rid of Santa Claus or the Little Mermaid. But we do need to teach our children what the word *truth* means. Truth is fact. Truth really happened.

Always use the Bible. Even if you're not reading from the text, have the Bible open in your lap so preschoolers will know what you're saying is coming straight from the Bible.

Encourage older preschoolers to bring their Bibles. Take time to show them how to open their Bibles to the exact page you're reading from. They love this and it helps them grasp God's truth in a more concrete way.

Let's be determined to use the gifts God has given us to teach our children about the unchanging truth of God's Word.

—Gina

33

Yeah! It's Worship Time!

I love the pure energy that erupts when our preschoolers gather in a group to experience God—it's one of my favorite times in ministry.

When we do our planning, here's how we build a worship flow that creates an amazing and age-appropriate experience for preschoolers.

Welcome (1 minute)—The host welcomes preschoolers and interacts with them. Make sure this person is a "big kid" who can inspire smiles, giggles, and cheers.

Song (2 minutes)—The worship leader leads children in a fun, energetic worship song with simple motions.

Bible verse (2 minutes)—The host teaches kids the Bible verse of the month. Keep the verse short; a single sentence works best.

Song (2 minutes)—The worship leader leads kids in a fun, medium-paced worship song with simple motions.

Bible Time (4 to 5 minutes)—An energetic person shares from the Bible, using audience participation and tools such as pictures, puppets, or props. He or she also has preschoolers repeat the teaching truth several times before, during, and after the telling. The teaching truth is based on the Bible and is a simple statement of a few words. An example would be "God watches over me" based on Noah and the Ark.

Prayer (30 seconds)—We close in prayer. Children can participate in the prayer by repeating each line. An example would be "Dear God (pause), thank you for watching over me. (Pause.) I know you're always with me. (Pause.) In Jesus' name. Amen."

Worship time can be the highlight of preschoolers' week when you create an experience they can connect with. I love it when parents tell me...

- how much their children love coming to church.

- how their preschoolers talk with them about what they learned in worship.

- how their children sing songs during the week that they learned at church.

I love it when I walk by an environment and see preschoolers saying by their actions and enthusiasm, "Yeah! It's worship time!"

— **Dale**

The Word is living and active and brings true transformation to the hearts and lives of people. Can you imagine trying to venture through this life without it? I'm truly thankful for the gift of God's Word.

We're here to share the true stories of God's love with the next generation. We're the communicators. And it's vital that we make the most of this opportunity. After all, we only have the preschoolers for a short time each week. Here's how to increase the impact of your Bible time.

Emphatically remind preschoolers that the Bible is God's book. Take every opportunity to convey to preschoolers what they hear from the Bible is God's truth, given to us by God. These aren't made-up stories. Always treat the Bible with special respect to show preschoolers this isn't an ordinary book.

Tell, don't read, the Bible. You don't necessarily have to have the Scripture memorized; just know where you're going and hit all the main points.

Use expressiveness. Make it exciting. God's Word is too awesome to be shared in a boring way.

Offer concrete experiences. Let kids pretend they're inside the furnace with Shadrach, Meshach and Abednego; let them taste, see, and feel the bread that Jesus shared with the 5,000. For example, a couple who teach 4- and 5-year-olds in our preschool ministry once brought in 12 large baskets filled with loaves of bread. There must've been close to 100 loaves of bread in the room that day. It was a very dramatic illustration for the preschoolers, not only to see that God will supply all our needs, but also that he'll often give us more than we need. That's a lesson they'll never forget.

Our children need to hear the wonderful truth of God's love, mercy, and amazing grace. Let's be committed to telling them in a way that captivates their hearts and communicates truth so they can understand. And just maybe your preschoolers will be saying, "Tell it again!" this Sunday.

—Gina

35

The Cure for Puppet-Phobia

Puppets are the cockroaches of our preschool ministries...they'll exist long after all of us are gone.

While this may sound as if I have something against puppets, it's not entirely true. When puppets are used professionally and creatively, they can grab kids' attention and open them to learning God's truth. Puppets can be engaging, and kids typically love them. Puppets are still one of the top tools used by churches to teach preschoolers the Bible.

The thing that bothers me about puppets, though, is that most preschool puppet shows aren't performed professionally and with excellence. Many of the puppet shows I've seen performed in preschool ministry resemble a bad foreign film where the mouths of the characters don't sync with their words and actions.

Up until a year ago, we'd stopped using puppets in our preschool ministry because our use of puppets fell into the "really dreadful" category of puppet shows. Today we don't have a formalized puppet ministry per se, but we've started using them on occasion. Two primary ideas have revitalized the use of puppets in our preschool programming.

1. We create and edit most of our puppet shows using video. With the use of green screens, we can make our puppets appear anywhere we want them to be. And if we don't like the sketch, we can simply shoot it again until we get it right.

2. We prerecord all the voices. This allows our puppeteers to focus on one thing: the movement and interaction of the puppets. Everything is in sync because our puppeteers aren't trying to memorize scripts and manipulate puppets at the same time. We've also found that the volunteers with the best puppet voices aren't necessarily the best puppeteers. By prerecording the puppets' voices, we can match each volunteer's role with his or her greatest skill.

These changes have brought a level of professionalism that's cured our church's former puppet-phobia. We've discovered that, if done right, puppets are a tremendous help in teaching preschoolers truth.

—Eric

36

The Needs of the One

Children with special needs represent a unique challenge to the church because Christian education is far behind the American public school system.

Since Congress passed a mandatory education law in 1975, schools have been required to provide free and appropriate education for every child. A part of this law is the LRE (Least Restrictive Environment), which ensures children are to be educated in the classroom with their peers. Also, since the passing of the ADA (American Disabilities Act) in 1990, people with disabilities are ensured the right to move easily through their communities with no hindrance to transportation, communication, or employment.

As a result of these changes, parents now come to church and rightly expect the same help their children receive from public schools. But are we prepared?

Meeting the needs of a child with a learning or physical disability can be very challenging, but never is this more apparent than in a preschool ministry. While some children have evident physical disabilities or are born with a condition such as Down syndrome, many other conditions such as attention-deficit hyperactivity disorders or autism spectrum disorders can't be diagnosed until children are 4 or 5 years old. This often leaves a preschool department guessing as to how to provide the best Christian education possible for every child. As strong as the temptation may sometimes be to make a diagnosis, it's not our job. Rather we are to work with the parents and child and make sure all children are equally welcomed in the church.

Here are some ideas for making sure your preschool ministry provides a welcoming environment for children with special needs.

- **Speak with the parents.** If you're having trouble with a child and believe you could be dealing with a learning disability, carefully address this with the parents—without bringing up your suspicion of a disability. Instead, approach this conversation from the standpoint of finding the right environment for the child. Maybe the child's current preschool ministry room is too restrictive and he or she needs a more developmentally appropriate environment. Ask parents to help you place their child where he or she would receive the best attention and ministry. Removing a child from a room without parental permission can cause anger, and the family may leave the church.

- **Check for dietary restrictions.** If you don't already have a child information form in place, do so as soon as possible, and get one filled out for every preschooler. This form should include an area for diet restrictions. Children who are undergoing testing for possible learning disabilities are often on wheat- and milk-free diets. Make sure your snacks or food experiences don't violate these diet restrictions.

- **Have buddies available.** For children who need special attention, whether diagnosed or not, assign learning companions who'll stay with them during your preschool ministry. Let parents know—they're aware of their children's challenges and welcome help.

- **Make sure your curriculum is developmentally appropriate.** Developmental appropriateness is important for all preschool ministries. If your curriculum meets the needs of all learning styles and preferences, you won't have to worry as much when it comes to adapting your curriculum for children with special needs.

- **Have special seating ready for preschoolers who need it.** You'll need to have special chairs for any child who's developmentally delayed due to cerebral palsy, Down syndrome, or any other physical disability. There are many products on the market today that can be used to transform traditional chairs into chairs that meet children's special needs.

—Barbara

Each week our preschoolers enter a world where the Bible comes to life. The various stage areas in our current preschool building include an aquarium, a cityscape that looks like a town in Jerusalem, and an outdoor scene—but a little more than a year ago, we didn't have anything that resembled a preschool worship area for large group experiences.

We were in an old building that housed our nursery and preschool ministries. We had no space. All our rooms were maxed out. We didn't have a stage; we didn't have worship teams; we didn't have creative Bible teachers. When it came to multimedia, we were more no-tech than low-tech. So how did we get from where we were a year ago to where we are today?

First, we started with the end in mind. We knew that our end goal was to teach preschoolers in a large group worship environment. We also knew that we couldn't wait for a new building to implement our strategy. So we started a preschool large group experience long before we had a preschool large group area. We started with two volunteers, a CD player, and a rolling cart. Our "large group" team would rotate to each of our preschool ministry rooms to teach the Bible and lead the kids in worship. We didn't let our humble circumstances keep us from our ultimate aspiration.

Next, we cast a compelling vision of our preschool ministry's future. We needed to build our volunteer team of creative Bible teachers, actors, and worship leaders. We knew this required recruiting people with the specific skill sets to teach preschoolers in a large group setting. To do that, we had to paint a picture of what it would be like to lead preschoolers in worship and use drama and creativity to influence their spiritual growth.

Keep in mind that we couldn't cast a vision using a large group area because we didn't have one. Our vision had to be compelling enough to inspire volunteers to begin with our room-to-room model and help us lay the foundation for things to come. By casting a powerful vision, we were able to build a solid team. When we finally moved into our large group space, we didn't miss a beat.

Don't let the fact that you may not have a large group area for preschoolers keep you from designing an unforgettable experience for your ministry. No matter where you are right now, know your strategy and start with the end in mind. Then recruit volunteers to that end by casting a compelling vision of what can be.

—**Eric**

The Greatest and Truest Story

Stories capture preschoolers' attention and hearts, and they're not alone. People of all ages love stories. Each year people all over the world spend billions of dollars to hear, see, and experience stories. Stories are part of our very DNA. We're wired to connect with stories because we're part of God's story unfolding here on earth.

Jesus was the master storyteller. Much of his teaching was done through stories called parables, and people flocked to hear him. Great communicators are great storytellers.

Tell stories well, and...

- you'll grab the hearts of preschoolers.

- you'll effectively communicate God's truth to preschoolers.

- you'll keep preschoolers on the edge of their seats.

- parents will drive across town to have their children be a part of your preschool ministry.

How do you make your preschool ministry a place where great stories are told? Remember, it's about the presentation. The Bible contains the greatest true stories ever told—and the greatest stories deserve the greatest presentation. Here's how to give 110 percent to present them well.

Raise up great storytellers. Don't just put anyone on stage. I've made this mistake, and in just a few minutes the kids were completely disengaged. Look for people God has blessed with the gift of communication. Cultivate this gift in them, and teach them how to go from being good storytellers to being great storytellers. Here are a few guidelines I use to grow storytellers.

- **Involve the audience in the story.** Great storytellers invoke participation and involve everyone. For example, in telling about David and Goliath, bring up two people to play David and Goliath. Then have each half of the room represent one of the two armies.

Dramatically guide them through acting out the story while you tell it—except for using a real rock for the slingshot!

- **Describe the scene.** Paint the picture of what it looked like. For David and Goliath, an example would be, "It was a gloomy day. On one side of the valley stood the army of Israel. Across the valley on a rocky hillside camped the army of the Philistines."

- **Describe the characters.** For example, "They were staring at a giant man named Goliath. He was *sooo tall!* His giant spear was like a tree trunk, and he had a huge shield that carried the marks of battles fought and won."

- **Vary your voice.** Use different voice levels to bring excitement and tension to the story. For example, *(whispering)* "Suddenly the Israelites saw the biggest, strongest man they'd ever encountered walk to the edge of the hill. He raised his hands to his mouth and shouted to them *(loudly)*, 'Who dares to come and fight with me?' "

Use pictures to enhance stories. It's true that a picture is worth a thousand words. The mind reads pictures much faster than words. Using pictures when you tell a story will immediately enhance it. Even in our high-tech age, storybooks still work well with preschoolers. Kids love to gather around a book for Bible time. Use Bible storybooks that have lots of pictures.

Use videos and DVDs as a format for storytelling. Movies and DVDs are simply stories. That's why children love watching them. I don't recommend going totally video, but I do recommend alternating video with live storytelling or using a combination of the two.

Use puppets to tell stories. Preschoolers love puppets. Puppets can bring life and energy to a story.

We've just opened a new children's building. The hallways are designed with storefront buildings that represent Bible stories: Jonah's Travel Agency, Esther's Day Spa, Goliath's Big and Tall Shop, Solomon's Bank, Joseph's Coat Shop, Rahab's Rooftop Inn, and more. Each building has a brochure holder containing cards that describe its Bible story. Parents can walk up to a building, pick up a card, and talk about the story with their children.

Our prayer is that the greatest and truest stories ever told will be passed from one generation to the next.

—**Dale**

The 'So What' Factor

I have a confession to make. It's probably not the confession you'd expect from a children's pastor, but I'm going to share it anyway. It may even seem a little sacrilegious, but...I didn't like church when I was a kid.

As a child, my family and I were "Chreasters," which means we only attended church on Christmas and Easter. Even with my limited church experience, I really didn't look forward to the days we had to go to church.

One of my earliest memories of church occurred while I was in pre-kindergarten. I was watching an episode of *Super Friends* when my dad told me it was time to go to church. I reluctantly got dressed and off we went. Instead of letting me sit with them in "big church," my parents dropped me off in Sunday school.

I remember the teacher had us gather around her on the floor for circle time. Then she told us something from the Bible about a guy who was thrown into a lion's den and lived to tell about it. The other kids seemed to know this really well because they could recall all the details from memory. I have to admit, it seemed like a cool story. But I thought to myself, *So what?* Sure, the lions didn't eat the guy, but I never really understood the point. For me, it was no different from watching the Super Friends defeat their enemies in *Legion of Doom*.

How many preschoolers leave our ministries each week asking themselves the same question: *So what?*

- They may be able to recite the Bible story verbatim, but they're missing the point of the story.

- We may be teaching them the story of Daniel, but they fail to notice the point of Daniel's obedience to God and his trust in God no matter what happened in his life.

- Our preschoolers may love the story of David fighting a giant but never grasp that it was God's power working in and through David that killed Goliath, not David's accuracy with a slingshot.

If we want God's Word to change the lives of the kids in our preschool ministries, we have to answer the question "So what?" before we can teach them to apply the Word.

Our preschool ministries need to help kids develop heart attitudes, motivations, and actions that are in line with God and his Word. We have to help them move beyond learning God's story from the Bible to living out God's story in their daily lives. If we can accomplish this each and every Sunday, our kids will gladly turn off their cartoons and come to church to learn how God wants to change them from the inside out.

—**Eric**

Lessons From Playhouse Disney Live

How do you engage preschoolers and their parents? Visit Playhouse Disney Live at Disneyland or Walt Disney World and you'll discover the answer.

Preschool families love shared experiences, and that's what you'll find at this 22-minute live show designed for preschoolers and their families. You'll see preschoolers and parents singing, dancing, and having fun together. You'll see parents thrilled that their children are having so much fun, and preschoolers smiling and enjoying a special moment with Mom and Dad.

Plan shared experiences for preschoolers and parents that include the following elements—and families will come!

Interaction—Interaction is a key element at Playhouse Disney Live. The host has the children shout out their names, say the magic words so the clubhouse will appear, help look for a character, cheer for characters, and constantly help. Use lots of interaction instead of having children sit passively. When children are involved, they're engaged!

Movement—There's lots of dancing, moving, and motions. Preschoolers love to move...they were made for it. You can fight it, or you can guide it into positive expression. Give preschoolers lots of opportunities to move.

Puppets—Puppets appear throughout Playhouse Disney Live. The voices are prerecorded, and excellent puppeteers provide the action. Puppets capture preschoolers' attention.

Songs—Music and songs are an integral part of the show. Preschoolers join in, sing along, and do the motions. The songs are fun, peppy, and happy. Engage preschoolers with fun, happy, peppy worship songs.

Bubbles—In one part of the show, bubbles come down by the thousands... and the children love it! Get a bubble machine; they're not that expensive. Use it and watch the smiles appear.

Video and lights—Video images are projected and lights flash throughout the show. Preschoolers love videos and fun lights. Plan ways you can incorporate both into your experiences for preschoolers and their families.

Fun, bright colors—The stage and set at Playhouse Disney Live are decorated with bright colors. Decorate your preschool area with kid-friendly colors.

Happy, energetic leaders—An energetic, happy, college-age girl hosts Playhouse Disney Live. Her smile and fun spirit connected immediately with the preschoolers. Look for leaders who love being with preschoolers and are full of energy.

Stories—The show told stories; several of the puppets were involved in telling a story. Preschoolers love stories, and we have the greatest true stories ever told.

Variety—Playhouse Disney Live knows that preschoolers have very short attention spans. Every couple of minutes something new grabs kids' attention. The stage set transforms several times. No segment goes longer than a minute or two. A song...a puppet coming up...a video image bursting out...a light change...everything moves quickly. For 22 minutes, short attention spans are continually reset and held.

If you're ever at Disneyland or Walt Disney World, stop by Playhouse Disney Live to pick up even more tips on capturing the attention of today's preschoolers—as well as their parents' appreciation.

—**Dale**

Making Every Moment Count

On average, each child in our preschool ministries likely receives less than 90 minutes of our time and attention each week. So how do we make sure every second we have with each child counts? These simple concepts stated 2,400 years ago by Confucius are still relevant today:

I hear and I forget. I see and I remember. I do and I understand.

To create lessons that stick with children, we need to turn our preschool ministries into learning experiences where kids are actively learning and not just being passive receivers. The latest brain research tells us that children learn best when they're involved with their whole bodies—seeing, hearing, touching, tasting, and smelling. When planning a lesson, let the curriculum be a tool that can help you, but don't let it stifle your creativity. Instead think in terms of teaching through the senses. You'll end up with a more effective preschool ministry and children who'll enthusiastically tell their parents about their experiences—plus you'll feel more enthusiastic about teaching.

Each week ask yourself these questions as you prepare:

- **What does it look like?** This can be very simple. For example, teach the lesson to your preschoolers in a tent, or throw a blanket over a table and have all the children climb underneath. Use simple visuals such as light sticks and glow-in-the-dark stars, or create amazement by adding red food coloring to water to turn it into "wine." Thinking in this manner enables you to break free from the one-dimensional trap we so easily fall into.

- **What does it smell like?** Some researchers say that inhalation is the most direct route between the outside world and our brains. There are many ways to incorporate the sense of smell into your lessons. If you're teaching the lesson of Abraham, Sarah, and the three visitors, bring in fresh, hot food, such as lamb, so kids can experience enticing aromas. Scents are available in many forms and can be a fun way to turn your environment into part of the story.

- **What does it feel like?** Don't underestimate the importance of the sense of touch. Use items such as lambskin or deerskin. Or if you're teaching about a blind man, blindfold children and have them use their sense of touch to identify items in a bag.

- **What does it sound like?** Music is a "free ride" in learning that greatly enhances our retention of information. Use songs to help preschoolers learn Bible stories and biblical principles.

- **What does it taste like?** We usually give our preschoolers a snack, so why not make sure it reinforces the lesson? Let kids taste foods that are mentioned in the lesson, or use food to illustrate an element in the Bible. For instance, represent the Red Sea with red-colored gelatin, and let kids have fun eating while you discuss the Israelites' escape from Egypt.

—**Barbara**

42

Passing Traditions 'Up'

It happened more than 15 years ago, yet I remember it as if it were yesterday. I was a brand-new pastor, and one of my preschool teachers was going to be out of town on Sunday. None of our substitutes were available, so I decided to cover the preschool ministry myself. I thought, *How hard can this be? Three-year-olds are really cute and seem harmless. This will be a blast.* Somehow my mind pictured a room full of well-behaved preschoolers who'd sit "criss-cross applesauce" in a semicircle, eager to study the Bible and participate in the activities of the day. So although I studied the curriculum, for some unknown reason I didn't think through how to engage the kids and manage the classroom.

As you can imagine, it was a train wreck. I couldn't get little Joey's attention long enough to get him to stop playing with trucks. Suzie wouldn't stop dancing around the room like a ballerina. And every time I gave the kids instructions, Billy told me, "That's not the way we do it."

Exasperated and at the end of my rope, I finally asked Billy, "If it's not the way, please I'm begging you to show me how you do it."

Immediately, he flashed the lights and started the kids in a chorus of "Clean up, clean up, everybody everywhere. Clean up, clean up, everybody do your share." And to my surprise, they did it. Then the entire group gathered around for circle time. Billy told the kids, "If you can hear my voice, clap two times." They did it again! Then he looked at me and said, "Okay, Pastor Eric, you may teach us the Bible now." Needless to say, that experience taught me more about engaging preschoolers than everything I learned in all my seminary training.

If you want to effectively teach the Bible, engage your kids, and manage your preschool ministry, then you need to establish weekly traditions and regular routines. I learned from little Billy that preschoolers like predictability. They want to know what's next and what's expected of them. Establishing routines and traditions helps provide structure and continuity for everyone.

As you think through ways to implement traditions and routines in your preschool ministry, consider the following:

Provide verbal and nonverbal cues to help preschoolers learn appropriate behavior. This could be a song, a rhyme, or any other experience that's used in a predictable and repeated pattern over time to set expectations in your preschool ministry.

Use routines to signal transition times. Many preschoolers struggle with transitions. They find it hard to move from one experience to another in a timely manner. Traditions and routines serve as reminders that it's time to stop one activity and move on to the next.

Remain consistent in using traditions and rituals. Be willing to stick with it until your preschoolers get it. This means you'll need to repeat rituals over and over again until kids understand and respond.

Routines and traditions will keep your preschool ministry running smoothly. They help set expectations, provide continuity, smooth transitions, and engage your kids so you can effectively communicate God's Word.

—Eric

43

Seed Planters & Kingdom Illustrators

In Jesus' parable of the mustard seed, he asks two questions that have huge ramifications for our approach to preschool ministry: "What is the kingdom of God like? How can I illustrate it?" (Luke 13:18). The answers to these questions define our role as preschool ministry leaders who genuinely impact children's lives. They teach us to be seed planters and kingdom illustrators.

Seed Planters—When describing the kingdom of God, Jesus says, "It is like a tiny mustard seed that a man planted in a garden" (Luke 13:19a). The first principle is this: We're called to be seed planters. The problem is that seed-planting results take time to show up. We'd much rather build programs than plant seeds. But when we plant the seeds of the kingdom of God in preschoolers' lives, those seeds can grow into mighty trees of faith. At our church we focus on planting two vital seeds that introduce preschoolers to God.

- **God is our creator.** Knowing that God is our creator teaches preschoolers to praise God for all that he has made. This helps them understand that they're not here by accident but that God has "wonderfully and fearfully made" them. Because God is our creator, he's worthy of our trust and obedience.

- **God loves us.** For our preschoolers to love God, they must know the love of God. Not only did God create the world, but "God loved the world so much that he gave his one and only Son" (John 3:16). Preschoolers need to know that they can have a relationship with God through Jesus.

Kingdom Illustrators—Illustrators bring words to life by painting pictures that engage us in the story. To become kingdom illustrators, we need to bring biblical truth to life for the preschoolers at our church.

- **Large group worship experience**—Our large group programming is designed to engage preschoolers through video, lights, sound, creative worship, storytelling, puppets, and drama to make a lasting impression on their lives. Each week includes a time where children express their love for who God is and praise God for all he has created.

- **Small group environments**—After the large group worship experience, preschoolers take part in a small group environment that's designed to help them apply God's Word to their lives. We reinforce the Bible story of the day through wild and wiggly experiences and meaningful connections with their friends and adult leaders.

We illustrate the kingdom by painting the picture of Scripture on the canvas of our kids' lives. We plant the seeds—and God grows them for a lifetime.

—Eric

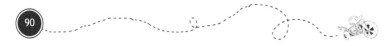

44

The Second-Service Solution

Ever been trapped in a boring situation where every second seemed like an eternity?

I remember two teachers at church when I was a child. They were equally boring. While one taught, the other one slept through the lesson, and vice versa. Wow...you can imagine how torturous it was for a young child.

Dé-jà vu—If you have more than one service on weekends, you probably face a dilemma: What about children who are there for more than one service because their parents attend one service and serve during the other? Many times kids have to go through preschool ministry again, which can lead to boredom, behavior issues—and dread. It's often the children of your most committed families who suffer. What should you do?

Boredom antidote—A few years ago, we got frustrated with this issue and came up with Kids' Place—a solution that's worked great for us.

Kids' Place is a room where kids can go when they're at church during a second service. Kids' Place doesn't have a structured lesson or schedule. It's a place where children can just hang out. Kids can choose from a variety of activities such as coloring, puzzles, crafts, board games, building blocks, video games, books, and more. We also provide snacks and drinks.

Children look forward to going to Kids' Place for their second service, and parents love it. It also helps us enlist many more volunteers. Some parents in your ministry may not be serving because they don't want their children sitting through the same experience twice. But when you provide a room like Kids' Place for their children, parents will be a lot more willing to serve. The time you spend enlisting volunteers for Kids' Place will be multiplied many times over by new volunteers who join your team because you offer it.

We want children to leave our services wanting more. We want them excited about coming back. A room like Kids' Place can be a key factor in making this happen.

—Dale

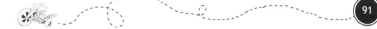

Flannel Graphs or MacBooks?

Clearly the times are changing—but what's the best way to reach preschoolers? The kids in our ministries are Digital Natives, children who've grown up with computers, the Internet, mobile phones, and MP3s as daily features in their lives. Rather than steering clear of technology in our preschool ministries, we need to use it to our advantage to relate to these children. But does this mean we need to replace books, games, and storyboards with video screens? Yes...and no. At our church we've adopted a high tech/high touch approach to preschool ministry.

High Tech—Our preschool department incorporates a lot of technology into our Sunday morning programming. Our preschool assembly room is equipped with state-of-the-art lighting, sound, and video equipment. Technology helps us add variety to our preschool ministry. The use of multimedia helps us engage our kids and get our message across to them in a relevant way. Video and sound effects help us appeal to preschoolers' sense of fun and excitement.

For example, when we taught our kids about Jesus calming the storm, instead of simply telling the story, we created a "storm" for our preschool large group experience. We used our light board to emulate lightning and sound effects to create thunder. We also used video of a thunderstorm on our projection screen. When Jesus calmed the storm, our video and sound effects changed as well.

High Touch—Believe it or not, we still use flannel graphs in our preschool ministry. However, we use them in our small group settings. We don't use flannel storyboards to teach the lesson, but we do allow preschoolers the opportunity to interact with each other and manipulate the storyboards in small group.

The majority of our preschool programming isn't based around the use of technology. The majority of our preschool programming is life on life; it's personal. It's built around small groups of preschoolers interacting with volunteers. We want preschoolers to build relationships and connect with each other and their adult leaders. Technology can't take the place of real volunteers interacting with real children.

Technology isn't a substitute for hands-on experiences with preschoolers. Dramatic play, crafts, circle time, and games are as essential as video in making God's Word relevant to preschoolers.

Technology and traditional methods of reaching preschoolers are *both* useful in initiating creativity, encouraging participation, and engaging our kids.

—Eric

Preschool Ministry Environment

Ready, Set, Grow!

Creating a playful, fun environment for preschoolers is a must for any preschool ministry. Think about this. An environment speaks to us. It projects a certain attitude or feeling. What's your preschool environment saying?

Does it say...*Fun! Excitement! We love preschoolers! Are you ready to play?* Or does it speak boring, drab words of apathy? No matter what size budget you're working with, you can create a preschool ministry environment that projects an attitude of fun and excitement.

Here are a few helpful tips for setting up rooms that attract every preschooler.

- **Set up play areas in different parts of the room.** Preschoolers feel like big kids when they get to make their own choices, and play areas allow preschoolers to choose the activities they'd like to participate in. Some examples might include a puzzle table, kitchen area, block area, and an art table with paper and crayons.

- **Set up play areas that correspond with the Bible content for that day.** If kids are learning about Joshua and the battle of Jericho, you might want to have them act it out in the block area. Or maybe they're learning about Creation and how light came into existence when God spoke. Place flashlights in one of the activity centers, and use them to create a memorable experience for kids. Remember that preschoolers learn using all five senses. Don't be afraid to try new things.

- **Set up rooms before preschoolers arrive.** You might be thinking... *In a perfect world! My volunteers constantly run late; we'd never be able to pull this off.* But we've found a simple solution to this problem. We've recruited volunteers specifically to set up the rooms for us on Sunday mornings. This ensures that all the rooms are ready for play by the time the first preschooler arrives. It's been one of our greatest ideas.

Don't be caught with a preschool environment that's saying all the wrong things. We want our preschoolers coming back for more. Look with fresh eyes this Sunday, and make the necessary changes to put your preschool ministry on top. The payoff is worth it.

—Gina

Honor Thy Ratios

Ever seen the reality show called *18 Kids and Counting*? It follows the Duggars, a family with 18 children at the time I'm writing this. When I served at a church in northwest Arkansas, the Duggars lived right next door in a small house. When I say small...it was small for a family that big. They'd occasionally visit our church and fill up a whole pew.

That many children in a small space may make for a good reality TV show, but it doesn't make for a good preschool ministry environment. When it comes to space and adult-to-child ratios, it's important to follow set guidelines. I've been blessed to be part of dynamic, growing churches over the years. When you're growing so fast you can barely keep your head above water, it's easy to let ratios slip...but it's not wise. "Pack 'em in with a grin" shouldn't be your motto. Following ratio guidelines will allow you to sustain the growth.

For leader-to-child ratios, here's what we follow at our church.

3-year-olds: 1 to 8

4-year-olds: 1 to 8

5-year-olds through kindergarten: 1 to 10

Here's what happens when you honor your ratios.

- **Effective learning takes place.** You can move from "crowd control" to interactive, hands-on learning.

- **Safety is increased.** You meet fire code regulations. Leaders can supervise children more closely, which leads to fewer accidents. You can more efficiently follow fire evacuation plans.

- **Leader retention goes up.** Nothing will burn out leaders faster than putting them in rooms where the ratio is out of proportion. They'll leave frustrated, and even the best leaders will wonder if they can do it again next week. When you honor your ratios, you're honoring your leaders. You're making their ministry doable and rewarding.

- **Parent confidence increases.** It puts parents at ease when they see a proper ratio because they know their preschoolers get stressed when they're put in crowded situations without enough toys, attention, and space for play.

So what do you do when you start exceeding your ratios and classroom sizes? First, you rejoice that God is entrusting you with new families. Second, you have to make a decision. You can close rooms once they reach capacity and invite families to take their preschoolers to a parent room, or you can start new classrooms. I'd not recommend closing rooms for very long. Proactively work with your senior leadership to come up with answers and make room for growth. It might mean starting a new service, asking families to switch to a less-attended service, or building more space.

Recently our preschool ministry grew quickly in just a matter of months. Classrooms exceeded ratios, and I knew something had to be done, so we came up with a plan to open three new preschool rooms. We enlisted the new team members we needed, and in a matter of weeks we were ready to open the new rooms. This gave us the space we needed to continue ministering to preschoolers with proper ratios.

The tyranny of the urgent sometimes causes us to push aside ratios and space issues. Many times we're just trying to survive by having classrooms open and staffed week by week. We realize rooms are overcrowded but don't deal with it. God doesn't want us to just survive, though; God wants us to thrive. He wants preschoolers to be in environments where they receive effective ministry. Let's work hard to honor our ratios and create environments where preschoolers can discover all God has for them.

—**Dale**

Emergency Evacuations: Are You Ready?

Your preschoolers are safe and secure in their rooms when suddenly the fire alarm goes off. What happens in the next few minutes will either be a catastrophe or a success. If you're prepared, it may still be a scary event, but people will know their jobs, follow the steps outlined, and more than likely, save lives. If you don't have an evacuation plan in place, begin this process at once.

Evacuating preschool children is a task that requires organization, information, training of staff and teachers, parent awareness, and special supplies. First of all, you need to give a written plan to your staff, teachers, and parents.

Your plan should provide specific details on the following:

Emergency Alert—How will everyone become aware of an emergency? After an alarm sounds, never silence or reset the fire alarm system until the fire department gives permission.

Evacuation Routes—Post primary and secondary evacuation routes on a wall in every room. Contact your local fire department if you need help planning these routes.

Evacuation Method—How will you evacuate the children? The best method is to line up preschoolers and have them hold on to a rope. Place one adult at the front and one adult at the back of each rope to ensure safety. Nonwalkers need evacuation beds. Always locate preschool rooms on the ground floor.

Post-Evacuation Plan—Designate an assembly area that's at least 100 feet from the building. Every teacher needs to bring an attendance sheet and make sure all the children from the room have arrived at the assembly area.

Once your plan is documented, equip each room with the needed supplies.

It's important to have a backpack containing emergency supplies so the teacher's hands will be free. Label the backpack "Emergency Supplies," and hang it directly below a prominently placed emergency procedures sign. Inside the backpack have a tarp, water bottle, flashlight, rope, latex gloves, bandages, paper towels, and wipes.

Each room needs a large printed list of steps for adults to take in an emergency. Remember to keep it simple. In an emergency, calm, clear steps can prevent panic. Your sign can be as simple as this:

EMERGENCY PROCEDURES

1. GATHER CHILDREN

2. BRING ATTENDANCE SHEET

3. BRING MAP DESIGNATING EMERGENCY ROUTES

4. BRING BACKPACK

Now you're ready to conduct practice drills. Begin with leaders and then practice with everyone, including the preschoolers. If you have questions or concerns, contact your local fire marshal for advice. For codes on exit requirements, you can search online for the Life Safety Code published by the National Fire Protection Association, or contact your state's Department of Human Services for plans on the evacuation of day care centers.

—Barbara

Parent-Friendly Preschool Spaces

When it comes to designing our preschool environments, we typically focus on making our spaces kid-friendly. We spend most of our efforts on how to decorate and theme our rooms so they'll appeal to kids. We're diligent about choosing colors kids like and age-appropriate toys. Yet we often overlook one of the most important audiences for our preschool environment—parents.

Of course, parents want our preschool ministry to appeal to their kids with an attractive, fun space. They want décor and themes specifically designed for their children. But for parents to really appreciate all the hard work we put into designing our space, it's got to appeal to kids while targeting parents. Here's how to do just that.

Sweat the small stuff. After designing and building three different preschool ministry environments at our church, I know the temptation is to finish the décor and theme and think you're done. The truth is that's only the beginning. You need to give thought to the following...

- Your check-in process is part of your preschool environment. Is it parent-friendly? Check-in should be fast, safe, and easy to do with a 3-year-old in tow.

- The height of the sinks and the size of the potties speak volumes to parents. We've found that parents also like it when we place the coat hooks at a level where their preschoolers can pick up their own coats. This may not seem like much, but little things go a long way with parents.

- A small side note on color: Be kid-friendly without being parent-repulsive. We use fun, bright colors but our preschool space never looks like McDonald's. We always choose colors that are at least three or four shades away from primary colors. This way preschoolers still love the color scheme, but parents are attracted by it as well.

Keep it fresh. An additional way to make your preschool environment appeal to parents is to make it fresh. Let's be honest, preschool ministry can easily become cluttered. Keep your area organized and clutter-free. Insist that the facility is clean.

Regularly go through the preschool rooms and toss out old games, torn books, broken toys, and the rest of the junk that can accumulate in a preschool environment. Then replace all the old books, games, and toys with new ones. Buy nice storage containers for all your preschool toys. Constantly look for ways to freshen and tidy up.

Our preschool ministry environments must be kid-friendly. After all, it's for the kids. But by applying these two principles—sweat the small stuff and keep it fresh—we bring an element of appeal to our facility that attracts parents in big ways.

—**Eric**

What's That Smell?

Anyone involved in preschool ministry knows that smells can be a challenge, and I don't have to be specific to bring back a few "odor associations" as you read this. So be careful about your preschool ministry environment from parents' and children's point of view and smell, and welcome families by creating pleasant odor associations. There are many ways we can do this without utilizing typical odor-masking sprays that work by creating the absence of odor or, worse, by covering an awful odor with a powerful scent.

Remember that the sense of smell transmits messages directly to the brain's area of higher learning. To utilize this powerful tool, create an environment that's inviting and also intriguing.

Essential oils—Add a few drops of essential oil, such as lemon, lavender, or rosemary, to a spray bottle filled with water. Shake well and spray the room a few minutes before preschoolers arrive.

Food—If your Bible lesson mentions any type of food, add a food experience.

- If you have a bread-making machine, bake bread just before children come; then focus on a Scripture that talks about bread, and let children eat the fresh-baked bread.

- Telling kids about Jonah? Create instant atmosphere by placing an open can of tuna in a corner of the room.

  - If you're talking about Noah, have kids experience the colors of the rainbow through smell. What do these colors smell like? Purple could be grape jelly, red—strawberries, yellow—lemon, and orange—an orange.

Nature scents—Hunt up cedar discs at your local sporting goods store, and place them around the room for a rich aroma. A small amount of hay in a corner sets the environment for telling kids about the birth of Jesus.

Become a habitual "sniffer," and enhance your preschool ministry environment with one of the many fragrance options available. Have fun and keep parents and children coming back for more.

—Barbara

51

Labels That Stick

Every preschool ministry needs labels. As a matter of fact, I think labels should be as commonplace in your ministry as the preschoolers you serve. Think about it, labels help you know what you're dealing with. They allow you to create groupings in your ministry. Labels help your volunteers stay one step ahead of the kids in their classrooms. I'm not talking about the kinds of labels we sometimes put on kids—I'm talking about the kind we create with a label maker.

In our preschool ministry we label everything. We use labels to keep us organized. They take the guesswork out of finding resources. Labels make replenishing supplies a breeze. Our volunteers love them, and I'm convinced our preschool director couldn't live without them.

- **We use labels to organize our resource room.** Our resource room serves as supply central for our preschool volunteers. Everything we need from crepe paper and cleaning supplies to string and Silly Putty is located in our resource room. And here's the key...it all has a home. Everything (and I mean everything) is placed in a bin, labeled, and alphabetized.

- **We use labels in our classrooms.** Our volunteers know where to find what they need when they need it because scissors are always in the bin labeled "scissors" and glue is always located in the bin labeled "glue." Even our toy bins and bookshelves are labeled with words and pictures showing where things belong. This is extremely helpful when it's time to clean up our toys and get ready for crafts or story time because our kids can help us clean up. Not only does this help the next group that uses the room, but our kids also enjoy matching the toys to the correct bins.

- **We use labels to help us set up on Sundays.** Each week we have a volunteer team that comes in and gets everything ready for our preschool ministry. They pull all the needed craft supplies, resources, and snacks for our upcoming lesson. Everything's labeled, so they don't waste their time searching for supplies; they can tell us what needs to be ordered, and they can ensure everything is ready to go on Sunday morning.

I know this seems simple, and it is. Every preschool director needs a label maker. As a matter of fact, a label maker will become one of your best friends in ministry. Labels will turn you into an organization guru and eliminate the stress of looking for what you need on Sunday morning. They'll also free up your volunteers to spend their time serving preschoolers, not searching for scissors.

So get busy making labels as commonplace as kids in your preschool ministry.

—**Eric**

Safety First

If we surveyed 100 parents and asked them the #1 thing they look for in a preschool ministry, it's safe to say their greatest concern would be the safety of their children.

This absolutely can't be compromised. Parents must be able to trust caregivers. Only when there's trust will parents feel confident about bringing their children. I've seen families leave churches because of one incident where a child wasn't properly taken care of. Kids will be kids and accidents will happen. But we can take these steps to ensure that our preschool ministries are safe, sound, and ready for preschoolers.

Create a manual of written policies. The more clearly and concisely you can state your policies, the better. No one wants to read a 150-page policy manual. Hit the most important policies, and communicate them effectively in written form. Get input from a team of parents and volunteers to help create your policies.

Communicate safety policies to all volunteers. Hold a meeting with all first-time volunteers, and make sure they clearly understand all safety rules and regulations.

Communicate safety policies to your leaders regularly. Every time you connect with your leaders via email or newsletter, highlight a safety policy. These little reminders will go a long way. We do this seasonally. For example, when the weather warms up, we send out a reminder about playground safety rules; when the weather gets cold, we send out reminders about health issues, colds, runny noses, and hand sanitizing.

Enlist nurses to volunteer their time. If you have church members who are RNs, ask them to be on call when they're attending worship or adult classes during times kids are in preschool ministry. You need to be able to reach these volunteers quickly and efficiently.

Here are a few rules of safety that are must-do's.

- Have safety gates or Dutch doors in all rooms. Children shouldn't be able to exit rooms on their own.

- Cover electrical outlets with safety plugs.

- Remove broken toys, small toy pieces, toys with small magnets, and sharp objects from all rooms.

- Make sure furniture is child-friendly and safe for preschoolers. Ensure that large furniture items such as bookshelves are firmly anchored so they can't tip over.

- Tape down rugs so there's no hazard or possibility of tripping.

- Provide volunteers with environmentally friendly sanitizers for hands, toys, and surface areas.

- Make sure rooms have adequate heating and cooling.

Take these steps and you'll be on your way to a clean, safe environment for your preschoolers.

—**Gina**

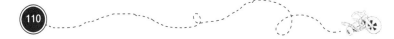

Show Us Your Sign

My wife and I took our three kids to one of Florida's many tourist attractions on a recent vacation. Being a first-time visitor to this particular park and a parent of two preschoolers, one of the things that impressed me was the park's use of signage. As you know, the last thing you want to have to do with preschoolers in tow is to stop, pull out your map, and try to figure out where you are and where you need to go next.

The park we visited was made up of five general areas. Signs easily directed us to specific areas, and then signs within each area pointed us to the specific attractions we were looking for. Not one time during our visit did we need to stop and ask directions or consult our map.

This park's use of directional signage set us at ease and enhanced our family's experience. I think some of the same principles can help us enhance the experience of families who visit our preschool ministries.

Signs need to effectively move people. The first principle I learned is that the main goal of signs in a public place is to direct people to where they need to go. Efficient signage moves people from the general to the specific. Families visiting your preschool ministry don't have time to stop by a welcome center and ask for directions. Remember, they're traveling with preschoolers. They need to be able to easily and quickly determine where they're going and the direction they need to go to get there.

To move families from the general to the specific, place signs for your preschool ministry at every decision point. For example, you need general signage at every entry into your building that points families to your preschool ministry. Once families find your preschool area, their next decision is to find their child's room. So you need specific signage pointing families to each of your age-graded rooms.

Signs need to be highly visible. The second principle I learned is that if you can't see the sign, it's useless. For your signs to be seen, there shouldn't be any barrier between the placement of your signs and the user's line of sight. This means that in your lobby or preschool hallway your signs need to be above the crowd.

Readability is another important factor in ensuring your signs can be seen. Use easy-to read fonts for your signs. Make sure letters are big enough to be seen at a distance. A common rule of thumb is to use a ratio of 25 feet per inch of text. This means that a 1-inch font can be read 25 feet away; a 2-inch font can be read 50 feet away, and so on. Additional considerations include eye-catching colors, the use of contrasts, and simple images to help families see your signs.

Good signage in our preschool ministries will create a positive, user-friendly experience for your visitors. It'll lower their anxiety, help them feel self-sufficient, and increase their ability to move throughout your facilities. So as you design your signs, remember that signs move people and need high visibility.

—**Eric**

Organize, Organize, Organize!

The average room in a preschool ministry will have six to eight children—and more than 200 supply items. Keeping these items organized, labeled, and easily accessible is a challenge that can't be taken lightly. No matter how excellent your curriculum or adult leaders may be, a disorganized environment creates failure and frustration. Keeping teaching materials, craft supplies, and general supplies well-organized allows leaders to spend their time with the kids instead of searching for needed items.

Use large cabinets. Have two large cabinets anchored to the wall in each preschool ministry room to contain supplies: one for leaders' supplies and the other for craft and general supplies. This keeps supplies off the floor and out of sight until they're needed—especially important if you're sharing the space with other ministries. Then follow these steps to keep the cabinets organized and resupplied.

- Label the shelves to identify what belongs on each one. Clearly mark items in boxes or bins so volunteers don't have to open them to know what's inside.

- Take photos of the shelves when everything is perfectly organized, and post these photos inside the cabinets. This will eliminate uncertainty about how cabinets should look at the beginning and end of each preschool ministry session.

- Post a "reminder" checklist of frequently restocked items, and provide small notepads so volunteers can jot down which supplies are running low and turn in written requests. As a backup to this resupply strategy, find someone who loves to organize, and invite this person to serve one day every other month to give the room a big-picture look for items that need to be replaced. Enlist this person or another willing volunteer to actually make needed purchases.

Explain the organization system. When you have volunteer meetings or orientations, include an explanation of the organization system you've created for preschool ministry and the reasoning behind it. Afterward take the time to stop by the rooms and ask if volunteers have any questions or needs.

Show understanding. Never criticize anyone for not keeping everything exactly the way you've pictured or requested. If you've done everything possible to organize and simplify things for people, you won't be faced with this situation often, but there'll still be occasions when a room isn't left to your desired standards. Many times people will need to pick up their children, meet their families for worship, or need to leave quickly for some other reason.

Keep it clean. Enlist a group of volunteers to give the preschool ministry room a deep cleaning every few months. Even if your church has a cleaning crew, many areas need extra attention.

—**Barbara**

Centers Are Central

Anyone who's ever worked with preschoolers knows they can be a busy bunch. Preschoolers really enjoy playing in groups with their friends, and they're constantly moving from one activity to another.

During these years, preschoolers' free play is becoming much more structured as well. They can go from group interaction to individual play and back to group interaction at a moment's notice. Learning centers in our preschool ministry rooms can transform potentially chaotic situations into organized, fun, and highly intentional learning environments.

At our church we set up three primary learning centers each week to reinforce what kids are learning and foster an environment for intentional learning. We use these centers during unstructured times such as parent drop-off and pick-up. We also encourage children to participate in learning centers as they finish planned activities so everyone can work at his or her own pace. Each of these centers is designed to expand learning in our preschool ministry.

1. Manipulatives Center—This center gives preschoolers opportunities to learn to think for themselves, make decisions, and recognize the rights of others. It includes various building materials, blocks, puzzles, and lacing cards.

Our manipulatives center is built around the two S's: simplicity and spaciousness. First of all, we keep it simple, but we provide enough variety so it's not boring. Second, we keep it spacious. This center requires enough open floor space so kids can work alone or in groups.

2. Home Living Center—This area is designed for community. The home living center enhances our kids' relationships with peers by allowing them to interact and role-play with each other. The center includes kitchen appliances, play food, dishes, pots, and pans. Our preschoolers practice cooking and thanking God for the food he has given us. They can pretend to be various members of a family or practice friendship roles.

3. Creative Arts Center—We resource this area either for dramatic play or art projects, depending on each week's learning focus. Dress-up clothes encourage children to dress like people in the Bible and act out the events. Art projects can vary from finger-painting to making objects with modeling clay.

Centers are a great way to reinforce Bible learning. They encourage active participation because every child is involved in the learning process. They can be developed around all learning styles. They also provide preschoolers the freedom to choose what they want to do within the framework of an organized preschool ministry.

Once you implement learning centers, you'll soon discover that they're central to creating a fun, organized, and highly intentional environment for preschoolers to discover God's truth.

—**Eric**

Space: The Preschool Frontier

Did you know the rule of thumb for building a preschool facility recommends a preschool room be 320 square feet minimum, have 35 square feet per child, and include a sink and restroom in each room? For most of us in preschool ministry, this would be our dream come true. The majority of preschool facilities in churches fall far below these recommendations, though, so we're constantly looking for new and creative ways to maximize the space we have.

When planning your space, take into account the social, emotional, and intellectual characteristics of 3-, 4-, and 5-year-olds, and design your space around their requirements. Here's what preschoolers need in their space.

Attractive rooms—Preschoolers respond to inviting environments. Paint the walls with light colors to make the room appear larger; then add pictures or murals to provide extra interest and brighter colors.

Orderly rooms—Use cabinets and shelves, and add hooks for hanging coats and backpacks. Keep shelves and cabinets well-organized and clean.

Multiple areas—Every preschool room should include two different group settings: tables and chairs in one area for crafts and other table activities, and one area with a large rug or individual carpet squares for Bible time.

Consider these additional concepts to make sure you're maximizing space in the most efficient way.

- **Make rooms easily identifiable.** For example, you can designate preschool rooms by flying flags near the doorways. If you need to change rooms for any reason, you can easily move flags. Whatever identification system you use, create something recognizable for children and adults. Preschoolers can't read, so signs need pictures and words.

- **Place rooms in consecutive order by age.** Random layouts can be frustrating for parents and children—don't make people wander the hallways. After you've planned your space in the least confusing manner possible, get feedback from adults who don't have preschoolers by challenging them to find specific rooms.

- **Design versatile rooms.** You'll restrict the use of rooms if you design them in a permanent way around particular curricula or ages. You'll encounter times when some age groups are larger than others, so keep rooms flexible, and invest in age-specific items that are easy to move.

—**Barbara**

57

Child-Size Me

I'm writing this on a flight from Atlanta to West Palm Beach. Two rows in front of me, an 18-month-old screams for his mommy. The young lady on my left is tossing and turning as she tries to take a nap. My colleague and I are both trying to work on our laptops. We keep bumping elbows as we type. To see the computer screen, I have to sit straight up and strain my neck to see what I'm typing. My knees are embedded in the seatback in front of me. Oh great, the gentleman directly in front me just decided it was a good idea to recline his seat into my lap. I have a feeling that working isn't going to work. I'm cramped, I'm uncomfortable, and nothing seems to fit right. The seat is too small, the legroom is too narrow, and it just doesn't fit me. Like the 18-month-old two rows up, I want to scream.

It's clear that airplanes aren't designed to be office substitutes. They're not conducive for working. The environment isn't nearly as inviting as the local coffee shop in my hometown. When the engineers at Boeing designed this plane, they didn't sit around and put my comfort and ability to get work done at the top of their list of necessities. Let's be honest, I'm not sure they put comfort on their list at all.

I wonder how many preschoolers feel the same way when they enter our preschool ministries. I'm sure they're thinking, *The chairs are too big, the table's too tall, and it just doesn't fit me.* Unlike Boeing, we do need to think first and foremost about our children when setting up our preschool rooms.

There are three criteria we use to determine if a preschool room at our church is child-sized.

Accessibility—First of all, specific things in our rooms need to be accessible. Can the kids reach the sink? Are the table and chairs preschooler-friendly? Is the tallest shelf on the bookcase reachable by a 3-year-old?

Practicality—Second, everything needs to be practical. For example, are the toys age-appropriate? It's probably not a good idea to give your preschoolers a 1,000-piece jigsaw puzzle. Do you have rugs for kids to sit on during story time? Can a 4-year-old easily complete your crafts in the allotted time?

Visibility—Finally, everything needs to be visible. Is everything at eye level for a preschooler? Are your toy bins clearly labeled with the name of the item in the bin and a corresponding picture so kids can identify what they're looking for? During Bible time, can you make eye contact with all the kids? Be sure they can see you and engage with you.

By ensuring that everything in your preschool environment is accessible, practical, and visible, you're designing a place with kids in mind. A child-sized preschool room is inviting and comfortable and just the right fit for the kids in your ministry.

—**Eric**

58

How Green Is My Preschool?

We use cleaners containing chemical disinfectants to stop the spread of communicable diseases in our preschool ministries—but when we douse our tables and toys with these products, we're replacing germs with toxins. Preschoolers' bodies are developing and growing rapidly, and even small amounts of a chemical may impact a child's ability to reach his or her full potential.

How do we make our preschool area green and still provide a clean, germ-free environment? Use environmentally friendly disinfectants and cleaners. Many are now available for purchase, but why not make your own?

Grapefruit Seed Extract—Add 20 drops of grapefruit seed extract to one gallon of water. Use in spray bottles.

Eucalyptus Oil—Add a drop or two to a damp cloth, and wipe down surfaces. Or if you use a sponge, make sure it's made of natural materials because essential oils react with plastic.

Vinegar—Plain vinegar (5 percent acidity) cleans 99 percent of bacteria, 82 percent of mold, and 80 percent of viruses.

Hydrogen Peroxide and Vinegar—*Warning: Don't mix these two ingredients together in a single container!* Hydrogen peroxide and vinegar each work effectively to kill bacteria, but they work even better when you spray one first and then the other. You'll need two separate spray bottles. Fill one spray bottle with 3 percent hydrogen peroxide, the same strength available at the drug store for gargling or disinfecting wounds. Spray on surfaces, allow it to act for 30 seconds, and then wipe down. Fill another bottle with plain white vinegar, spray, and wipe the surface with a clean cloth.

Borax—Mix ½ cup borax into 1 gallon of hot water to disinfect and deodorize.

Vinegar and baking soda—Dissolve ½ cup vinegar and ¼ cup baking soda in ½ gallon of water for an excellent cleaning agent. Store and keep on hand.

Isopropyl alcohol—Use alone as a disinfectant.

Baking soda—Cleans, deodorizes, and scours.

DON'T USE:

Aerosol sprays—These may contain propane and formaldehyde (a carcinogen). Aerosols have been linked to the dramatic increase of asthma in children.

Bleach (sodium hypochlorite)—Found in a wide range of household cleaners, bleach is hazardous to people with heart conditions or asthma and can be fatal if swallowed. Bleach has been linked to learning and behavioral problems in children.

Antibacterial soaps and hand sanitizers—The overuse of these items has been linked to the emergence of resistant strains of bacteria. It's best to use warm running water and soap.

Nontoxic cleaning products represent a new level of hospitality we can offer to the children who've been entrusted to us.

—**Barbara**

59

From Distraction to Interaction

When I first came on staff, our preschool ministry looked like a graveyard for unwanted toys. With the best intentions, church members would donate their used, unwanted, and sometimes broken toys. I remember arriving early one Sunday morning to find seven large trash bags full of old toys sitting in our hallway. As a result, we finally faced up to this challenge.

Clutter and Chaos—Mounds and mounds of toys of all shapes, colors, and sizes cluttered our rooms. It was nearly impossible to organize our preschool ministry because there weren't enough bins at the Container Store to house all the toys. Our children played with a hodgepodge of misfit toys—everything from remote control cars without the remotes to kitchen sets without cooking utensils. Some rooms had really large LEGO tables, and other rooms had no LEGO toys at all.

Not only were the rooms disheveled, but our kids were also distracted. They'd rather play with toys than engage in the Bible story. This overstimulation caused hyperactivity in some kids, while others were overwhelmed by the multitude of choices. It was like trying to teach a lesson in the middle of FAO Schwarz. Our leaders were constantly luring preschoolers away from the toys in an effort to teach them the Bible. Something had to change.

Rescue and Renovation—One of the first people I hired on our staff was a preschool director who helped transition us to a less-is-more philosophy for our preschool rooms. She knew that if our goal was to help volunteers interact spiritually with preschoolers, kids needed to be less distracted with toys. Here's what she did.

- First of all, she began the audacious task of uncluttering our toy bins by responding with a flat-out no to all donations.

- Next, she grouped all our toys into those we could use and those we could trash. Then she tossed out all the toys that were broken or had missing parts, and she replenished our rooms with the toys we could keep.

We've experienced amazing results since implementing a minimalistic approach to toys. We're now extremely intentional about the toys we place in our rooms.

- Our rooms and toys are set up around learning centers. If a toy doesn't fit into one of our learning centers, it doesn't fit into our preschool ministry.

- We rotate certain toys based on what kids are learning each Sunday morning. This keeps our rooms fresh and keeps kids from getting bored with the same old toys every week.

- Preschoolers transition more easily to worship, craft, and Bible time because they're not over-stimulated by an unlimited supply of toys.

And ultimately, our volunteers experience much more spiritual interaction with preschoolers, which was our goal all along.

—Eric

Go Big With Décor

When we teach about Creation in our preschool ministry, we tell our preschoolers that when God created, he made something from nothing. He didn't use glue, paper, scissors, or crayons. He spoke and everything we know, and even what we don't know, came into existence. God has given each of us a share in his creative power, and we can tap into this when we're planning our preschool ministry environments.

You may say, "Wait just a minute. You haven't seen my budget. I'd love my preschool ministry area to look like Disneyland; I just don't have the resources." But we serve a God with unlimited resources, and you can do a lot on a limited budget.

Follow these suggestions to get from where you are to where you want to go.

Form a design team. Find the most creative people you know—put an ad in the church bulletin calling all artists and creative people. You'll be amazed by the response you get.

Hold a brainstorming session. Discuss ministry names, theme ideas, perhaps even a Bible verse that describes the heart of your preschool ministry. Get as detailed as possible. Put together sketches, color renderings, and layouts. You can't have too much detail.

One question that always comes up is whether to focus on the hallways or the rooms. My personal advice is to do the hallways first. Less is more when it comes to the interior of the rooms, but do what you and your team think is best for your ministry.

Put together a workable plan and a budget. You may need to spread this project out over several months or even a year. Do what you can. Get as many volunteers as you can find to do the painting and any necessary repairs—this can save thousands of dollars. Also it never hurts to ask a local paint store for discounts. There may even be someone in the church who works at a paint store. You won't know until you ask.

Set a deadline and get to work. It's always amazing to see God's people come together and work toward a common goal. Focus your prayer during this time on how faithful God is and how he is the ultimate giver of all good things.

Have a party. Celebrate your newly decorated facility with a grand opening. This is great way to create synergy and bring new life to your ministry. Advertise this event to the community as well. Go big!

Make your preschool ministry a fun place for worship and learning...a place preschoolers will look forward to coming to week after week.

—**Gina**

Preschool Ministry Volunteers

4 Things Your Preschool Volunteers Need

> **"Their responsibility is to equip God's people to do his work and build up the church, the body of Christ."**
>
> —(Ephesians 4:12)

If you're going to build an excellent preschool ministry, you have to know how to build a strong team of preschool volunteers. You can be great with preschoolers, but until you build and lead an excellent volunteer team, your preschool ministry will never reach its full potential.

Your responsibility is to equip the leaders who in turn minister to the preschoolers. Your ministry to your volunteers is just as important as your direct ministry to the children. Does that mean you don't have any classroom time with preschoolers? Absolutely not. But if you're the primary person doing the preschool ministry on weekends, you're greatly limiting the ministry, and you'll quickly hit a wall. Show me a great preschool ministry, and I'll show you a great team of empowered volunteers who are doing the work of the ministry.

As you equip and lead your volunteers, here are four things they need.

1. Connection—People want to serve in community. They want to be known and build relationships with the people they serve alongside. Joining your team is like becoming part of a family. Start a Facebook page for your team. Encourage your team to connect outside of the time they serve. Get together and participate in fun activities. No training allowed at these times. Just hang out and enjoy each other.

When people are connected, they grow together in their faith. When people are connected, they stick around. When people are connected, they look forward to serving because they get to be with friends.

2. Care—Life is messy...full of ups and downs. And when you do life as a team, you go through things together. The people on your team are going to experience hurts, heartaches, tragedies, loss, and turmoil. When that happens, they need to be cared for. They need a shoulder to lean on...a hug...a prayer. There may be times they need meals brought to them or even financial support. They'll need your care.

But remember, you can't do it all. One person can only effectively care for four or five people. It's important to create a culture where your team cares for and supports each other. In our church we've raised up volunteer coaches. They call volunteers each week and check on them, support them through prayer, and encourage them.

Another great way to care for volunteers is to have a prayer huddle before the children arrive. Spend time each week sharing prayer requests and praying for each other.

3. Celebration—Your volunteers need to feel valued. Celebrate them! Let them know how much they mean to you. Celebrate not just what they *do* but who they *are*.

Every week in our staff meeting, we each take time to write a personal note to a volunteer. We let volunteers know what they mean to us and what we appreciate about them. At Christmas, we have a big party in their honor. At the end of our ministry year in May, we have another big party to celebrate them.

4. Challenge—Your volunteers want to grow in their faith and ministry gifts. You're called to help them grow. Make sure they're attending adult worship. Encourage them to be in a Bible study. Provide quality leadership opportunities that will propel their faith and gifts to new levels. Challenge them to step up in leadership responsibilities as you see them developing.

Your goal isn't to plug them into a spot where you have a need. Your goal is to help them grow in their faith. When you help them discover their gifts, equip them to do ministry with their gifts, and challenge them to continually grow, you'll fulfill Ephesians 4:12.

Once a quarter we send out an email survey to our team, using survey monkey.com. We ask these key questions to see how we're doing: Do you feel connected? Are you being cared for? Are you challenged? Are you celebrated?

We also ask for input and ideas on how we can serve them better in these four ways. We're doing well in some areas, and in other areas we have work to do. It's all part of the journey of helping our team of volunteers grow in their faith and gifts.

—Dale

Can You Hear Me Now?

Verizon Wireless once coined the phrase, "Can you hear me now?" If your family is anything like mine, you wore that line out. We still use it from time to time.

In my first few years of ministry, I'd get to the point of complete frustration because I didn't think anyone could hear me asking for help. We were growing at a rapid pace and didn't have a sufficient number of volunteers. The volunteers we did have were overworked and getting to the point of burnout. I wanted to march myself right into the worship center and yell at the top of my lungs, "Hey, we're dying here. Does anybody want to get up out of a seat and help? Yeah, I'm talking to you—can you hear me?"

But over the years I've learned that there are better ways to ask for help. I hope the following ideas will inspire you as you begin to get the word out to your church family that you're here and open for business.

- **Pray.** God's Word says, "The harvest is great, but the workers are few. So pray to the Lord who is in charge of the harvest; ask him to send more workers into his fields" (Matthew 9:37-38). His Word is clear. Pray for workers. I pray year round for workers, not just when we're in recruitment mode. God is faithful and true to his Word.

- **Get up-close and personal.** One-on-one is the best way to recruit volunteers. I rarely get helpers from an ad in the Sunday bulletin. Why? A 30-word ad can't communicate my passion; only I can clearly communicate my passion to another human being. This is key in recruiting.

- **Watch your vocabulary.** When asking for volunteers, refrain from using words such as "Volunteers wanted," "We're desperate," "Need help," "Looking for anybody," or "A caveman could do this, for crying out loud." When you use a negative approach, you project an attitude of desperation and the idea that any warm body could do this.

Instead use words such as "Our preschool ministry is growing," "We have exciting service opportunities available," "We have a place for you on our team," and "Want to make a difference on the next generation?" When using these words you're saying, "We've got it together, and we know where we're going. Want to go with us?"

Do you see the difference in this approach? People don't want to jump onto a sinking ship, but they just might hop onboard a ship that's going somewhere. It's all how you say it—but I know what you're thinking! You're thinking, *We are desperate!* I totally understand. But you can't let that be your battle cry. Your battle cry must be something like this...

"I'm called to influence an entire generation for Christ. I will not beg, kick, or plead. But by God's grace and the gifts he has given me, I'll put together the most passionate, sold-out team of preschool volunteers that ever walked the planet."

Now *that's* what I like to hear!

—**Gina**

Profile of a Passionate Preschool Volunteer

You can have every policy in place, the grandest facilities in the country, and a supply room that looks like the local craft store, but if you don't have volunteers who are passionate and qualified to serve preschoolers, your ministry foundation is shaky.

The key to laying this solid foundation is to understand the importance of enlisting the help of the right people. So what's the profile of a passionate preschool volunteer? Look for these five characteristics.

1. Christ Follower—Know for certain that this person has a relationship with Christ. You don't just want Christians; you want Christians who love God with all their hearts, souls, and minds. You want leaders who are passionate about getting God's Word into the hearts of children.

During your initial meeting, ask potential volunteers to tell you how they came to know Christ. Ask them to tell you how Christ has changed their lives. Look for excitement in their faces as they tell their faith stories.

2. Dependable–When I visit with preschool leaders across the country, over and over again they ask me, "How do you get people to show up? We have so many people bail out on us on Sunday." This is an unacceptable situation; you've got to be able to rely on your volunteers.

During the interview process, make sure people understand what's required of them. Sometimes leaders are afraid to raise the bar for fear potential volunteers will back away. Be clear about your expectations. Help them understand how chaotic it can be for preschoolers and parents when volunteers are late, and then ask this simple, point blank question, "Will you give me your promise that I can depend on you?"

3. Trustworthy—Parents are leaving their children in your volunteers' care, and parents need to feel absolute trust. Don't overlook this huge issue when you're looking at potential volunteers. Taking time to do background checks and reference checks is nonnegotiable.

You also need to ask every new volunteer if he or she has ever worked with preschoolers before. If so, get the "when" and "where" info, and make a follow-up call. It's important for you to know everything you possibly can about volunteers before you allow them to be with preschoolers.

4. Genuine love for children—When people have a natural love for children, it shows in the way children are drawn to them. They know how to get down on preschoolers' level and talk with them. I'm not saying this can't be taught. I'm just saying there are plenty of people out there who have a natural love for children and the ability to communicate with them.

One way you can determine if potential volunteers have this quality is to allow them to assist in your preschool ministry for a few weeks. Put them with your best teachers. Let them spend time interacting with children, and then ask your volunteer leaders to give you feedback. This one practical application has helped me more than anything else in determining how well someone will fit our preschool ministry.

5. Joyful heart—Have you ever received service from a cashier, waitress, or salesperson who looked as if he or she had just eaten a sour pickle? It always makes me feel like these people are bothered by me *personally* and wished they were somewhere else. Parents and preschoolers feel the same way when they're greeted by a volunteer who has no joy and looks as if he or she has no desire to be there.

Make your preschool ministry the happiest place in the church by filling it with the most joyful volunteers in the church. Don't compromise on this very important character trait. This is a quality that should be evident from the first moment you meet with a potential volunteer. You don't need to ask people if they have joy; you'll see it in their eyes and in the way they share their faith stories with you.

Stay true to this profile of characteristics, and you're sure to have a fired-up, passionate volunteer staff.

—**Gina**

64

The Power of the Spoken Word

The church is a place where the weary, downtrodden, broken, and bruised can find comfort, hope, and healing. Many families who enter the doors of your church each week are seeking just that. They're often dealing with strained marriages, uncertain job situations, and stress from everyday life. Some of the moms have been wrestling with their preschoolers all week. They're frustrated, tired, and ready for a breather. All they want is a pleasant drop-off for their children, a quick escape to the Sunday morning worship service, and a cheerful pick-up.

Nothing's more frustrating to parents than to drop off or pick up their children and have to interact with a volunteer who's decided to vent his or her own frustrations about life. Unfortunately, I've sometimes overheard remarks such as these...

Drop-off:

"I don't have any help this morning. I guess it's just me."

"Is he going to cry the entire time?"

"Wish I were going to the service with you."

"You had a bad week? That makes two of us."

Or maybe the volunteer doesn't say anything at all. That's the worst.

Pick-up:

"He cried the entire time."

"He didn't participate in any of our activities today."

"Caleb? We didn't have a Caleb here today. Oh, that boy. He was so quiet we hardly even noticed him."

"I am so ready to get out of here."

"I think your child has a developmental problem; you may want to get that checked out."

Words are powerful. They have the ability to heal or hurt, uplift or tear down, bring blessing or bring burden. As leaders it's imperative that we teach our volunteers the power of the spoken word. We're called to be salt and light. A single wrong word could possibly turn a family away from the church forever. As scary as that sounds, it's true. Think about what you say. Help your volunteers understand that every word they speak will either bless or burden a family. Here are some examples of how to speak words of love and affirmation to parents and children.

Drop-off:

"How's Caleb today? I'm so glad you're here."

"We're going to have so much fun today. Are you ready to play?"

"Enjoy the service. We'll take good care of Caleb while you're gone."

Pick-up:

"Caleb was such a blessing. You have a precious little boy."

"Caleb learned about Noah today. Ask him to tell you all about it."

"Thank you for sharing your little boy with us today."

I believe you can find something positive to say about every child. The spoken word is powerful. Make sure the words coming from your volunteer staff bring blessing and not burdens to the hearts of young families.

—Gina

Wanted: A Few Good Men

I hate to say it, but many of our preschool ministries are like a bad country song, "Where Have All the Good Men Gone"? A shortage of men working with little children has been a cultural trend that dates back to the time of Jesus: "One day some parents brought their children to Jesus so he could touch and bless them. But the disciples scolded the parents for bothering him. When Jesus saw what was happening, he was angry with his disciples. He said to them, 'Let the children come to me. Don't stop them! For the kingdom of God belongs to those who are like these children' " (Mark 10:13-14).

While this trend has been happening for a very long time, we've set out to change the cultural climate and recruit men to serve in our preschool ministry. I'd like to unpack our strategy for attracting, engaging, and developing men.

Attract—The first thing we do to attract men is to lead with vision. We cast a vision for what could happen if men invested their kingdom effort in preschoolers. Leading with a need is just the opposite. When preschool ministries lead with a need ("We don't have enough volunteers!"), their recruiting efforts focus on closing gaps in the schedule. Not only is this unattractive, but it also makes your preschool ministry come across as needy.

But when you recruit people to a vision, it creates buy-in. Vision shows men the value of volunteering with preschoolers. It paints a picture of the significance of men having an influence on young children's lives.

Another way we attract men to work with preschoolers is by actively targeting them. We do this by highlighting men who are already serving in our preschool ministry. We share stories with our senior pastor about men making a difference in the lives of preschoolers, and our senior pastor shares those stories with our church members through sermon illustrations.

Finally, we attract men by incorporating masculinity into our preschool ministry. We use masculine fonts, such as Arial Black, Impact, or other bold sans-serif fonts, in our promotional pieces and take-home sheets. A lot of our worship music has a masculine feel to it. Even our games and crafts have a male bent to them—we play high-energy games such as tag and relay races, and we do fun crafts such as making slime or mixing soda and Mentos candies to create explosions that illustrate God's power.

Engage—Once we've attracted men to our preschool ministry, we set out to engage them. We give men clear direction. We let men know where we're going as a ministry and how we're going to get there. Strong leadership also engages the men who are on our team. Some of the strongest male leaders in our church serve in our preschool ministry and continue to do so because we place a high value on leadership. We also engage our male volunteers, as we do our female volunteers, by helping them find their best possible fit on the team.

Develop—At one point, we found that men were leaving our preschool ministry team because we weren't providing them with the tools they needed to be successful. That's why we now focus on equipping men with the core competencies they need to thrive. For example, we teach men how to manage a classroom of preschoolers by establishing routines, developing a discipline plan, and keeping kids active during worship. We also teach our men to look for teachable moments so preschoolers can apply the lessons they're learning. We provide lots of feedback and encouragement because men want to know that they're making a difference. They want straight talk about how they're doing. They want to know where they're succeeding and what areas they need to work on.

I'm confident that as you apply these principles to attract, engage, and develop men in your preschool ministry, you'll begin singing a new tune... "It's Raining Men"!

—**Eric**

Making Disciples? Sweet!

"We need 10 people to teach our preschoolers!"
"Please serve so our children can learn about God!"
"Come help us teach the next generation about Jesus!"

Sound familiar? The problem with these statements is that they focus on what people can do for your ministry instead of what your ministry can do to help people grow in their faith. We're called to make disciples. This means we're called to help people grow toward full devotion to Christ. When our focus shifts from filling holes to making disciples, we'll see our preschool team grow numerically and spiritually.

Here's how to make the shift...

- **Enlist people one-on-one.** There's no substitute for asking God to lead you to people, one at a time, whom you can invest in and help grow spiritually. Every Christian is created to serve; every Christian has a role to fulfill. Ephesians 2:10 says, "For we are God's masterpiece. He has created us anew in Christ Jesus, so we can do the good things he planned for us long ago." We have the awesome privilege of helping people discover the work God has prepared for them to do. This happens one person at a time.

- **Help people realize their gifts and talents.** First Corinthians 12 tells us that all Christians have been given one or more spiritual gifts. God has also given people talents and abilities—as we help people discover and use these gifts and talents, they're able to grow in their faith.

- **Find out people's passions.** I ask people what gets them excited. What dreams has God placed in their hearts?

- **Place people in their sweet spot.** When people are placed in their sweet spot based on their gifts and talents, they'll thrive and feel energized instead of drained after preschool ministry each week. We all have days when we're tired and want to stay home, but when we're in our sweet spot, we love what we're doing!

- **Give them permission to move if they're not in their sweet spot.** There are people who've served for years in the wrong position. They keep on serving in that spot because they're afraid they'll be called quitters or they'll let someone down if they stop. They dread serving. What a travesty! Encourage people before they join your preschool team to let you know right away if they end up in a position that's not their sweet spot. If they don't have that freedom, then one of two things will happen: They'll burn out and quit, or they'll endure years of drudgery and miss what God has wired them to do.

- **Check back with them in a month.** Four weeks after volunteers start serving, follow up with them and find out if they're serving in their sweet spot. This moves the previous point to the next level. Take the initiative and find out if they need to move to a new position.

- **Help them grow spiritually.** Invest in the spiritual lives of the people on your team. Make sure they're serving from the overflow of what God is doing in their lives. Serving on your preschool ministry team is a source of spiritual growth for all your volunteers.

- **Care more about them than just what they *do*.** People can sense when they're being used to do a job. If someone on your team looked tired, would you encourage him or her to take a few weeks off? Do you ever call the people on your team just to see how they're doing? Do they know they can come to you with personal prayer requests? Show you care first and foremost about each of them as a person.

Recently I interviewed a man who'd been asked to join our preschool team by another volunteer. He was ready and willing to join, but as I talked with him, it became clear that God had gifted him to work with teenagers. Sure enough, when I asked him what his dream job at church would be, he responded, "To help teenagers grow closer to God...but I'm willing to help with preschoolers if there's a need." I could've placed him in a preschool position, but I wouldn't have been helping him find his sweet spot. And I doubt he would've lasted. His discipleship was more important than filling a role. I asked if he'd rather serve where God had called and gifted him. He smiled and said, "Yes." I walked with him over to our student ministry and connected him with our student pastor.

I know Sunday's coming. And you have spots you need filled immediately, but take the long view. Shift your focus from just filling those spots to making disciples. God has people who'll thrive as disciples by serving in your preschool ministry. Be committed to discipleship, and God will bring you disciples!

—**Dale**

67

It's Personal

How well do you know your volunteers? Do you know the names of their children and their spouses, where they work, their hobbies, their stories? Here's what *I* know for sure: When you take the time to get to know your leaders on a deeper level, they'll go the distance with you.

You can't get to know someone in 10 minutes on a Sunday morning. Volunteers are busy teaching; you're busy leading. So use Sundays as an opportunity to ask volunteers if they have any available time for lunch the following week.

Meet for lunch. Lunch works great for one-on-one time or meeting with a couple. (Special Note: You should never have a lunch appointment where you're alone with a member of the opposite sex.) Lunch provides a more intimate setting than your office, so you can engage in a deeper, more personal conversation. These meetings aren't about you; they're about the volunteers. Let them tell you about their lives. Ask how you can pray for them. Let them know you appreciate them and are thankful they're on your team. And pick up the tab!

Open your home. My husband and I love to open our home to preschool volunteers. We sometimes have three or four couples at one time for dinner. We try to choose couples who might enjoy getting to know each other. Not only does this help you get to know your volunteers on a more personal level, but it also gives them a sense of being part of a family.

Often in ministry we get so caught up in the unimportant that we overlook what's most important. It's really quite simple...give an hour of your week for a volunteer, and he or she may very well repay your church's preschool ministry with a lifetime of service.

—**Gina**

Thanks a Million

Don't let the volunteer staff you've worked so diligently to gather fade away because of frustration and discouragement. Every person on the planet wants to feel valued and appreciated, and it's no different with your preschool ministry volunteers. Showing your appreciation will help them know they're making a difference. Try these ideas.

Hospitality cart—Offer volunteers a hospitality cart with juices, soft drinks, and doughnuts. They can stop by, grab a quick snack, and head to their rooms.

Handwritten thanks—Take time to write handwritten thank you notes. No email or texting here—just a note to let someone know you're thankful for the gifts he or she brings to your ministry.

Help at hand—Enlist a hallway coordinator to check on each room every 15 minutes or so. Volunteers will appreciate knowing there's someone close at hand to help them with anything they might need.

Happy affirmations—My team has a lot of fun expressing appreciation in novel ways. Here are a few ideas we've used:

- Roll of mint-flavored Life Savers candy—"You're worth a mint to our preschool ministry."

- Package of gum—"It's *refreshing* to see your smiling face each week."

- Sonic Drive-In gift cards—"Every hour is 'happy hour' with you on our team."

- Microwave popcorn— "Thanks for popping with excitement over preschool ministry."

- $5 gas cards—"Thanks for going the extra mile."

- Krispy Kreme free doughnut card—"Our volunteers are the 'Kreme' of the crop."

- Starburst candy—"You bring a burst of color to preschool ministry."

- Starbucks gift cards—"You're the 'caffeine' in our ministry. Thank you for your energy and enthusiasm."

- Christmas ornament—"You decorate our ministry with goodness and grace."

- Six-pack of Double Stuf Oreo cookies—"You've got all the 'stuff' that makes our preschool ministry sweet."

- Car wash gift card—"You put the 'sparkle' in our preschool ministry."

- Jar candle—"Thank you for sharing the light of God's Word with our preschoolers."

- Individually wrapped muffin—"There's 'muffin' better than having you on our team."

- Package of hot cocoa—"Your warm heart is a blessing to our preschoolers."

If you haven't told your preschool volunteers lately how much you appreciate them, get your team together today and come up with your own creative ideas. Take time to thank people and let them know what a blessing they are to the children and your church's preschool ministry.

—Gina

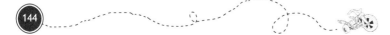

69

Supply and Demand

I love to cook, but sometimes I'll be right in the middle of putting together a great recipe only to realize I'm missing a key ingredient, and I'll make a sound kind of like, "Ughhh!" My husband recognizes this sound and yells from the living room, "Forget something?" Then he drives to our local market to pick up the needed ingredient, reminding me that he has his cell phone with him in case I think of anything else. I'm so thankful for this patient man.

Preparation is the key to success, and success can only happen when you have every needed resource at hand. In our preschool ministry we understand this principle, and it's our responsibility as leaders to ensure that our volunteers have everything they need to have a successful teaching experience.

I'll never forget what happened one Sunday morning after a teacher asked me for crayons. When I went to the resource room, I couldn't find any. It was embarrassing to have to say I didn't have crayons! Since then we've put practices in place to be sure we're never short on glue sticks, crayons, construction paper, and other essential preschool supplies.

Here's how to guarantee that every volunteer and child has what he or she needs.

Make it easy to request supplies. Provide a means for volunteers to communicate what supplies need to be replaced. Have request forms and a drop-off basket or tray located where they're easily accessible; for example, in the resource room, in preschool ministry rooms, or in a central communication location for volunteers—or in all three places.

Honor special requests. Your volunteers may also ask you for special supplies from time to time. If it's within your budget, have these items ready for them when they arrive at their next teaching session.

Recruit a resource coordinator. In our preschool ministry we have a resource coordinator whose primary job is to get everything ready for the teachers each Sunday. Every room has a tub that she stocks with all the needed craft supplies and teaching tools. She even cuts out craft pieces for the younger preschoolers.

Yes, we do a lot for our teachers, but I've learned that most of them are so busy with their everyday lives they aren't able do ahead-of-time preparations each week. We want them to be successful. We want them and the children to have what they need, and we're committed to going the extra mile to make sure this happens.

Preparation brings success. Do what you can to help your volunteers be prepared. Remove as much of the burden as possible, so they can do what God has called them to do—put his Word into the hearts of preschoolers.

—Gina

I'm going to totally date myself here, but I grew up watching *Laverne & Shirley* and *Happy Days* every Tuesday night. I absolutely loved those shows. Laverne and Shirley were always getting themselves into the stickiest situations. Oftentimes they'd bicker and fight, but in the end they always came out as best of friends. Whenever they wanted to make sure the other got what was being said, one would say, "Get it," and the other would respond, "Got it," and then together they'd say, "Good." They were basically saying, "I've communicated some important information to you, and I want to make sure you understand." Get it, got it, good!—I still use this line with my children.

The way we communicate with leaders is changing. Gone are the days of weekly training meetings. Your leaders are only going to give you a few hours a week and much of that is going to be ministering to preschoolers. We used to have snail mail, land lines, and long, boring meetings. Now we have email, texting, and all sorts of social networking websites. I don't know about you, but I'm pretty much plugged in most of the time.

As leaders, we need to update our methods of communication. You might be saying, "But we've had training meetings every Sunday night since 1942." I say, "If that's still working for you, press on, brother." But if you're looking around and thinking, *Where is everyone?* maybe it's time to revamp your method of communication.

Here are a few suggestions that will have your volunteers saying, "Get it, got it, good!"

- **Do everything possible to avoid having a meeting.** We're "meeting obsessed," and most of our volunteer leaders have been in meetings all week at their workplaces. Another meeting is not what they're looking for. Ask yourself, *Can I say what I need to say through an email, text, or phone call?* If the answer is yes, then get to it. Don't fall into the trap of thinking you're not a good leader because you never have meetings.

- **Create attention-grabbing communication pieces.** If you want to remind your preschool leaders about an upcoming event, place a few Hershey's Kisses chocolates in a brown paper bag for each volunteer. Fold it, punch holes, and tie it with a bow. Attach a note card with a reminder about your event and any needs you might have. For example: "Don't forget, Blessing Bag Assembly Day. It's this coming Saturday, November 13th from 9:00 to noon. Join the preschool team as we come together to serve the young families in our community." What have you accomplished here? You've avoided meeting with volunteers to communicate information about an event. You've communicated effectively with an attention grabber, and you've blessed your volunteers with a little chocolate. There are hundreds of different ways you can communicate with your volunteers. Get creative.

- **Make meetings count.** If you absolutely, positively must have a meeting, make it count and make it count big. No one wants to show up for a meeting only to find out they were given information that could've been sent in an email. Most will leave thinking, *What a waste of my time. Note to self: Skip the next meeting.*

Meetings aren't the venue for imparting ministry information and key dates. They are, however, the venue for imparting your dream, vision, and heart for ministry. It's impossible to share this in an email. When you feel it's necessary to bring your team together and motivate them with the power of a dream, make it the best it can be. Go big or go home! You want your leaders leaving inspired, encouraged, and excited about getting back to their preschool ministries on Sunday.

—**Gina**

Preschool ministry can be a very demanding and stressful area for volunteers. Many volunteers will leave prematurely because of burnout caused by poor self-management, unrealistic expectations placed on them, or lack of support from leadership. Regardless of the underlying cause, the end result will be that a valuable volunteer has been lost for life.

One of the most important components of a preschool minister's job is the commitment to love and support volunteers in every possible way. It's essential to take notice of their time, their families, and the struggles they're facing in day-to-day life.

These simple practices will help you prevent volunteer burnout and keep a healthy and happy atmosphere in your preschool ministry.

- **Know your volunteers.** Take the time to develop a relationship with them in a nonprofessional setting. Find out about their families, their lives, their relationship to God, and their dreams for preschool ministry.

- **Set clear expectations.** There shouldn't be any questions about the job expectations for each volunteer. Create a job description that's clear and concise, and also set a specific length of time for his or her commitment.

- **Don't set up a volunteer for failure.** Some volunteer positions require more time and knowledge than others. Be careful to put the right person in the right job. If you place a novice volunteer into a position that requires experience, you're setting up that person for failure. Gradually work people into positions of higher responsibility.

- **Be willing to listen to advice.** No one has all the answers all the time. Your volunteers' observations can be invaluable, and you must always be open and willing to take advice. If your volunteers feel that you value their thoughts and advice, they'll develop an ownership attitude toward their positions and the preschool ministry.

- **Keep your volunteers motivated.** Provide training when possible, either within the church or at outside conferences. Everyone needs a "refresher," and the right training can renew the spirit of a volunteer on the verge of burnout.

- **Show appreciation.** The backbone of any preschool ministry is its volunteer staff. Always take time to say thank you, acknowledge the work volunteers have done, and remember their birthdays, anniversaries, and other important dates in their lives.

- **Be reliable and organized.** A volunteer's time is precious—don't waste it. Respond to their requests promptly. Follow through on your commitments, and keep yourself and your preschool ministry organized.

—**Barbara**

Preschoolers' Parents

72

In Line to See Santa!

I hate waiting in line, don't you? The ultimate misery for me is waiting in line at the department of motor vehicles. It's enough to drive you crazy—especially when you've moved to a new state and don't have a choice about standing in that line.

But I've watched preschool parents willingly stand in long lines. I've seen them stand in line for an hour just so their children could see Santa. I've seen them wait in long department store lines just so their children could have the popular toy that everyone wanted. I've seen them slowly weave their way through a maze of line stanchions so their preschoolers could go on a ride at a theme park. I've seen them wait in the summer heat so their children could have their photos taken with their favorite Disney characters. I've seen them wait patiently into the night so preschoolers could be part of a special holiday event such as Fourth of July fireworks. I've seen them stand in line to make their children's birthdays extra special.

All of that waiting was for one reason—so their children could have an experience that would create a wonderful memory. When I was a parent of a preschooler, I stood in those lines right along with everyone else. I wanted my boys to have fun experiences that would bring a smile to their faces and give them fond memories of their childhood.

So if parents are that committed to seeing their preschoolers have great experiences, we must ask ourselves this question: How can we create preschool experiences at church that'll have parents lined up to get their children in?

Why do parents wait in line so their preschoolers can see Santa and their favorite Disney characters? It's because kids have a relationship with these icons. These icons touch kids' heartstrings and foster happy memories. They touch the inner need of feeling loved by someone. What if your preschool ministry was full of volunteers who made preschoolers feel loved? volunteers who cheerfully greeted them by name each week? volunteers who created happy memories for them? I have some volunteers who are at this level. And parents and preschoolers can't wait to get to their preschool ministries each weekend. Parents will line up to have their preschoolers in an environment where caring leaders build loving, nurturing relationships with kids.

Why do parents line up to purchase the popular toy that everyone wants? It's because they want their preschoolers to have the very best. What if your church became known as the best place in town for preschoolers? What if the word spread that preschoolers were learning and living out biblical truths they were being taught at your church? What if unchurched preschool families saw the positive impact your church was having on families and this made them want the same for themselves?

Why do parents wait in long lines so their preschoolers can experience a ride at a theme park? It's because they want them to have a fun experience. When parents are on a ride with their children, you'll see them closely watching kids' expressions. They love to see their preschoolers' eyes light up with wonder. What if we created hands-on, interactive learning experiences at church that amazed preschoolers? What if we created worship experiences that lit up their faces with God's glory? What if we offered shared experiences where parents and preschoolers could have fun together?

Why do parents wait patiently so their preschoolers can be a part of a special holiday or birthday event? It's because they want to celebrate milestones with their children. What if we provide spiritual celebrations and milestones parents could experience with their children?

I recently witnessed something amazing. A mother was leaving church with her preschooler in her arms—and he was pitching a royal fit! He was trying to get away from her with all his might. He even had his take-home paper in his hand and was hitting her with it. I'll never forget what he was yelling—he was yelling, "No! I don't want to leave! No! I don't want to leave!" I'm not excusing his behavior. But my heart did rejoice that he'd had such a great experience at church that he didn't want to leave. I'd much rather our preschool parents had to drag their children *away* from church instead of *to* church!

My prayer is that half-empty hallways and classrooms will be a thing of the past for churches—that parents will line up to get their children into our preschool ministries. If we incorporate the strategies mentioned above, it can become a reality.

-—**Dale**

73

Partnering With Parents

We'd all agree that parents and the church play a significant role in the spiritual development of preschoolers. Scripture is clear that parents are their children's primary faith influencers. It's also clear that our preschool ministries have a biblical mandate to partner with parents. The question isn't whether we should partner with parents to train their little ones spiritually. The real question is what's the most effective way we can do this?

A recent study in Children's Ministry Magazine shed light on three main areas of connection between parents and the church, related to raising spiritually vital children.

Take-Home Handouts—While 54 percent of parents in the study identified take-home sheets as a helpful way for churches to partner with them, only 36 percent of parents actually used these handouts—which explains why you spend so much time recycling handouts at the end of each service.

At our church we set out to close the gap between parents' perceived value of handouts and the likelihood that they'll actually use them. On the back of our traditional take-home sheet we include "The Drive Home," three open-ended questions parents can ask their preschoolers on the way home to start a spiritual conversation about what kids have learned. We've found that our take-home sheets now leave our building and, at the very least, make it to the minivan.

We also know that our parents no longer have to settle for the pat answer of "Jesus" when asking their preschoolers what they learned at church.

Communication—The study found that 76 percent of parents preferred email communication and 35 percent preferred face-to-face conversations. Websites and snail mail were parents' least favorite forms of communication. This tells me that parents are looking for two-way communication about the spiritual development of their children, not simply one-way communication about what's happening in our preschool ministries. In other words, parents want to know *how* their preschoolers are doing, not *what* they're doing.

We train our volunteers to intentionally use drop-off and pick-up times to provide parents with specific feedback about their children's spiritual growth. We also collect stories from volunteers about individual preschoolers so we can include those stories in emails, text messages, and Facebook messages to their parents.

Training—Finally, the study discovered that parents aren't yet ready to fully embrace a "home-centered, church-supported" philosophy of family ministry. This shows me that parents need the church to provide training so they're more equipped to be the primary faith developers for their children.

Our church has set out to equip parents with a three-pronged approach of sermon series, workshops, and small groups.

- With the help of our senior pastor, we spend four to six weeks a year teaching biblical principles about parenting in our main service.

- We also provide at least one parenting seminar that's specifically geared for parents of preschoolers.

- Finally, we team up with our adult spiritual formation team to provide a 12- to 13-week small group study for parents of preschoolers that explores a biblical foundation for parenting.

While you may not be able to implement these specific strategies, our preschool ministries must take the initiative and help equip parents to be the spiritual leaders they're called to be.

—**Eric**

If I were to guess, social media is probably not the first thing that comes to mind when you think of preschool ministry. When it comes to youth ministry, using social media is a no-brainer, but let's face it, not too many 3-year-olds have Facebook pages. Yet Facebook is an invaluable tool for your preschool ministry because while the kids in your preschool ministry aren't on Facebook, it's more than likely their parents are. In fact, nearly 45 percent of Facebook users are ages 26 to 44.

Social media isn't going away any time soon, and with many parents of preschoolers using Facebook on a daily basis, it's imperative we learn how to maximize its influence in our preschool ministries. Facebook can open up a new approach to communications if we take advantage of the opportunity.

At our church, we've discovered Facebook provides a simple, easy-to-use tool that connects us with parents and allows parents to interact with each other. We've discovered that it's more effective than email, take-home sheets, and bulletin announcements to get our preschool message across to parents. Here's how to get plugged in.

Create a fan page. A Facebook fan page is a customizable profile that allows you to share and promote your preschool ministry with Facebook users. It can be created in just a few minutes using a simple interface. Here's a step-by-step guide to creating a Facebook fan page for your preschool ministry:

Step 1. Go to facebook.com/pages/create.php.

Step 2. Choose a category and name for your fan page. I recommend using the name of your preschool ministry and church when selecting the name. For example, we named our fan page, "12Stone Village: The Preschool Ministry of 12Stone Church."

Step 3. Add a profile picture. This can be the logo for your preschool ministry or the logo for your church.

Step 4. Add information. List your church address, service times, website, and so on for your fans.

Step 5. Publish your fan page. Click the "publish this page" link to share your fan page with the world. Oh yeah, don't forget to become a fan of your own page. And share it with friends by clicking the "share" button in the lower left of the wall or info tab.

Maximize your fan page. Make your fan page a useful resource for parents by updating your page with relevant and useful information—and posting on it frequently.

At our church, we update our fan page with an overview of what we're teaching preschoolers each month and a recap of what we teach each Sunday. By adding pictures and videos of our preschool ministry to our fan page, we've made it visually appealing. We've also enabled our fans to post their own pictures. We create photo albums of Sunday services and special events. We use our fan page to promote upcoming events and provide links to other parenting resources we find on the Web.

The sky's the limit as to what you can do with your fan page. The more content you add, the more parents can interact with your preschool ministry.

What started out as a novelty for us has turned into a very important tool. We've seen tremendous benefits as a result of creating a Facebook fan page for our preschool ministry.

- **Connection**—It's provided us with a deeper, more personal connection with parents. While email allows you to connect with people, Facebook is like email on steroids. Email tends to be formal and businesslike. But the informal nature of Facebook has made it easy for our parents to interact with our staff on a more personal level and opened up greater opportunities for us to minister to our preschool families.

- **Communication**—A Facebook fan page gives parents a single location where they can receive all the necessary communication from our preschool department. They discover what we're teaching, details for upcoming events, special announcements, and even volunteer opportunities. It's also opened up a line of two-way communication with parents in our ministry. Conversations are started both by our staff and our parents and benefit everyone. We're able to post questions and gain feedback...and our parents can do the same.

The bottom line is that you need to connect and communicate with parents in your preschool ministry—parents who are often strapped for time. You need to meet them where they are...and they're on Facebook. So set up your Facebook fan page, and watch it transform the way you minister to parents in your preschool ministry. It's free—and parents will follow you.

—Eric

Whether your preschool ministry includes five children or 500, it's the little things you do that demonstrate your love for the families entrusted to your care. What are these significant things that make a relational difference so parents keep coming back? Let's begin with the children.

- **Know kids by name.** Make preschoolers feel special and show you care for them by greeting each one by name and knowing something about their lives, such as their pets, toys, or families.

- **Show up when kids are sick.** Make a priority of visiting preschoolers when they're in the hospital or sick at home for a length of time. Bring a small gift, keep the visit short, and follow up if the illness is serious.

- **Acknowledge kids' birthdays.** Nothing's more important to a young child than a birthday. Mail an inexpensive birthday gift, such as a coloring book or other small item, and include a handwritten note. Enlist the help of seniors to shop dollar stores and help keep these gifts in stock. When you see the child, wish him or her a happy birthday.

- **Be a fun-loving kid at heart.** Dress up in costume when you can play a part at a special event, such as a princess tea, a cowboy barbecue, or a fall festival—or as someone out of the Bible to bring the Bible to life.

What can you do to strengthen your relationships when working with parents? The following strategies reinforce the fact that you care about them, too.

- **Relate to them nonjudgmentally.** At some point all preschoolers will misbehave, go through different stages of separation anxiety, or be problematic in some way. Never embarrass a parent over a child's behavior. If the incident is critical enough that it must be addressed, do so in private—not in front of other parents or the child.

- **Help parents disciple their preschoolers.** Parents are very concerned about their children's spiritual welfare or they wouldn't be at church. But many feel inadequate when it comes to teaching their children, and many have low expectations about what preschoolers are capable of understanding. Provide parents with resource lists and faith talks that help them lead their children spiritually.

- **Be there for parents.** If they're going through family struggles, let them know you're praying for them, and send notes of encouragement.

—**Barbara**

The Unhappy Parent: Handling Confrontation

No matter how hard you try, you'll encounter unhappy parents from time to time, and it'll be your responsibility to solve the problem in a manner that reflects God's love and your love for the children and families in your preschool ministry. How you deal with these confrontations will define your effectiveness as a leader. Try these ideas.

Don't take offense. We're all striving to do the best job possible, so when someone's unhappy with our ministry, it's easy to take it personally. Instead separate your personal feelings from the problem at hand, and keep your objectivity.

Listen carefully to the parents. If the parents are very angry, have them come to your office or a place where you can sit comfortably and discuss the incident. Take notes and document everything that's said. Don't be afraid to say, "I'll look into it" or "I'll get back to you." Often when parents understand and believe that their concerns are being taken seriously, you've already corrected half the problem. Set a time when you'll get back with them, and keep your commitment.

Research the problem. Speak in person with those who witnessed or were involved in the incident that caused parents to be offended. Listen to their description of what happened, and ask for their input on what can be done to prevent this from happening again—but don't do this in an accusatory manner. Never have this conversation on the phone or via email. This is a matter that needs to be dealt with on a personal level from all sides.

Seek the advice of leadership. Your church leaders have dealt with many confrontations and problems, so don't think it's a sign of incompetence to ask for their advice. It's actually a sign of wisdom to recognize those situations where you need help to resolve a problem.

Pray. Seek the advice and wisdom of God.

Address the solution. Once you've finished your inquiry, consulted those involved, and sought the advice of God and your leadership, meet with the parents again. Speak with them plainly and openly. Underestimating a person's intelligence is the worst thing you can do, and all of us can identify when we're being "handled" and will resent that fact.

Remember what's at stake: the permanent influence on a child and the parents' impression of your church. The solution must be sought with love and prayer.

—Barbara

77

The Welcome Wagon

With so many new technological advances in communication, our lives have become so complicated, stressful, and hurried that we're inclined to overlook the concept of personal connection.

While our predecessors considered a home visit to a new member or visitor an integral part of their workweek or volunteer commitment, we can come up with a dozen reasons now to avoid this vital aspect of preschool ministry. The most common excuse is that we don't want to impose on family time, or we feel too busy and think that sending a postcard, emailing, or making a quick phone call is an adequate welcome. And *adequate* is the correct word. While this long-distance approach might fulfill the technical requirement of making contact, it won't leave families feeling welcome and wanted.

Families who have preschoolers and are looking for a church home need to be assured of the ministry and care your church will offer their children. They need to meet the people they'll be entrusting with their children. Preschoolers are going to be apprehensive, and if they're scared of coming to your preschool ministry room, parents are unlikely to force them. Personally meeting and talking with preschoolers and their parents will be the greatest outreach you do in your ministry. To make these visits effective, call ahead to say you'd like to drop off some information, and then follow these simple guidelines.

1. Keep visits short. Don't make families feel pressured to invite you in. Simply introduce yourself, offer a quick description of the preschool ministry, and leave. If the family wants to continue the visit, by all means stay—but there's an art to making a visit short, purposeful, and nonintrusive.

2. Take a welcome packet with you. Include items such as a parent handbook, detailed information about the preschool ministry, a small gift for the child or children, information about adult classes and worship services, your business card, and information about any play groups or support groups that meet at your church. If a family isn't at home, leave the packet on the porch. Then make a phone call later, saying that you stopped to welcome them; offer to answer any questions they may have.

3. Speak to preschoolers, not just parents. If children are available, speak directly with them. Ask questions to show that you're interested in them and that they're important. If needed, make notes so that when you see children later, you'll be able to make personal references about their lives, such as asking how their pets are doing or how their soccer games went.

4. Offer to meet families at church and escort them to their rooms. When you do this, if children are feeling scared about being left, promise parents you'll personally keep a watchful eye and let them know if a child becomes upset.

5. Follow up with families. At this point a phone call is fine. Just connect to let parents know that you care and you're available.

—Barbara

78

Planting Spiritual Roots at Home

Family dynamics are very different from 25 years ago, and people now out-source what used to be considered family responsibilities—laundry, house-cleaning, daily care of children, and even home-cooked meals. People have also developed the habit of outsourcing their children's spiritual education. The family dynamic of building a basic spiritual foundation within the home is being lost. Without a doubt, this is the most critical issue that the church is facing today, and we need to work with parents of preschoolers to reverse this trend.

Our preschool ministries are uniquely situated to start young families off in the right direction to become active participants in their children's spiritual education. Parents of young children are eager to watch their children grow and develop spiritual foundations. Never is that opportunity more prevalent than in the preschool years of life, when children are entering a stage of self-awareness in which examples and stories of faith permanently influence them.

We must find ways to integrate our curriculum with home-based teaching that enables parents to interact spiritually with their children. This sounds intimidating, but you can develop these opportunities by giving parents resources that reinforce the lessons their children are learning in your preschool ministry. To begin this process, follow these basic steps.

- **Re-educate parents.** Many parents feel inadequate and need to build confidence and skills so they can take an active role in their children's spiritual growth. This requires your senior pastor's active participation through preaching that emphasizes parents' biblical responsibility to disciple their children, as well as resources that equip parents to lead faith talks in their homes.

- **Resource parents.** Suggest or provide family devotional books, create crafts that can be used throughout the week to reinforce

Bible learning, or develop your own take-home faith talks. These should follow your curriculum's scope and sequence and be designed for preschoolers' developmental stage. In fact, your curriculum should have simple papers that include the Bible lesson, questions for reinforcement, a song, and an activity that families can do together.

Learning biblical truth from their parents during these critical developmental years helps preschoolers lay a foundation for lifelong dedication to God.

—Barbara

79

Reaching Parents of Preschoolers

There are seasons of life when people become more open to God. One of these key times is when they become parents of preschoolers. Some parents had no spiritual upbringing, and they want things to be different for their children. Some of them walked away from faith in their college years. But now they're married...with kids. Young, innocent, inquisitive eyes begin to prompt them to give church another try. They realize it's time to come back for the sake of their children. They're in your city. How can you reach them?

1. Create a culture that's inviting to preschool families. If you want to reach parents of preschoolers, you must create a church culture that's designed for them. This is the number one way to reach them. You can have events and outreach, but if your weekly church environment isn't intentionally designed to reach preschool families, you'll have a difficult time reaching and keeping them. Here's how to create that culture.

- **A pastor who connects with preschool families**—A younger pastor may naturally draw preschool families, but regardless of age, a pastor who's willing to understand today's preschool families and meet their needs can effectively reach them; for example, through sermons relevant to their lives and music that connects with their generation—and most important by prioritizing preschool ministry.

- **A family-friendly preschool space**—Start in the parking lot with reserved parking for preschool families, and consciously design furniture, signage, and rooms so they're appropriate and inviting for preschoolers.

- **A greeting team that includes preschool parents**—Have preschool families welcomed by people who are in the same season of life.

- **An excellent preschool ministry**—It's simple...but so true. If their preschoolers love coming, parents will be back.

2. Partner with organizations that minister to preschool parents. Each week dozens of preschool moms come to our church through programs such as Mothers of Preschoolers (MOPS). Hosting parent-friendly programs is a great tool to reach preschool families.

3. Provide fun activities for preschool families. Preschool parents are looking for places to take their preschoolers. Your local McDonald's, playgrounds, mall play areas, Build-A-Bear Workshop stores, and so on are full of preschool families. What activities can you provide on a hot summer day or cold winter evening for them? Our church recently constructed an indoor playground. It gets hot in Florida during the summer, and we knew preschool parents would be looking for fun places with air-conditioning to hang out with their children. So we decided to open the playground for three hours on Tuesdays and Thursdays for preschoolers and their parents. We even provided a kid's meal for them to purchase. The response has been overwhelming. Last week we had an indoor picnic and movie night for preschoolers and their parents. Again, the response was overwhelming. Get with your team and plan fun activities for preschool families. It might be renting a bounce house, setting up wading pools and serving sno cones, or having a fall festival. Strategically plan and promote your event, and parents will come.

4. Pray for the big "mo." The big "mo" is momentum. It comes from not just what you do but from who you are. When you become a place where preschool families feel welcomed, nurtured, and supported, you'll see momentum build. Preschool families will be drawn to your church, and as they spread the word and bring other preschool families with them, momentum will move through your city to reach unchurched families.

A few weeks ago I was in our playground after the service. A mother approached me and introduced herself. Then she pointed out a father playing with his preschool son in the park and said, "That's my husband. For more than seven years I've been praying he'd come to church. When the playground opened, he finally agreed to come so he could play with our son after the service. He's been coming ever since and is listening. I know God is using our preschool son to draw my husband to him."

As I looked at that father and his son playing together on the playground, I thanked God our church is a place where preschool families feel welcome. And I'm believing and praying that God is going to reach that little boy's father!

—Dale

Being a parent of a preschooler is one of the hardest jobs on the planet. I remember those days of parenting. They were fun, cherished times, but they could definitely leave me frazzled at the end of the day. It reminds me of the preschool boy who asked his parents, "If you're tired, then why are you putting me to bed?" I was full of energy as a preschooler and quite a handful. I remember my grandfather once asking me, "Do you ever sit still?" And of course the answer was an emphatic "No!"

The only way I survived as a preschool parent was having my wonderful wife by my side. Together we navigated raising two preschool boys at once. I can't imagine raising them alone. It would've been more than twice as hard, I'm sure. But for many parents, that's the reality. They're raising preschoolers as single parents. The latest U.S. Census says there are 12.9 million single parents in America; 10.4 million are single moms and 2.5 are single fathers. My hat goes off to them.

Stop and think for a moment about the single parents in your church who have preschoolers. I'm sure many faces come to mind. You have a tremendous opportunity to come alongside them with support and encouragement.

Be sensitive to single parents' needs. Think about the single mom who's pulling into the parking lot. How can you make it easier for her? Reserved parking? Parking lot attendants to help with bags, strollers, and so on? Think about the single dad who has to take his daughter to the restroom. Do you have a family restroom where he can do this? Think about the single mom who's struggling financially because of her former husband's selfish choices. Can you help her financially? Recently a husband abandoned a mother in our church. He basically walked out with everything, including the car. She was put in a desperate situation. She had a job, but no way to get there. We found out and connected her with someone in the church who gave her a car.

Help single parents connect. Offer single parenting classes. Connect them with single parent small groups, women's ministry, men's ministry, and other opportunities to grow, relax, and make friendships. Offer free child care during these times. All parents need a break from their preschoolers—especially single parents.

Offer support to single parents' preschoolers. Many single parents welcome people who want to invest in their children. This is especially true when a single mom has a son with no father figure in his life. Consider starting a mentoring program in your church that connects these boys to Christlike men.

Jason (not his real name), who's 5 and attends our church, is struggling. I know why. His father recently walked out on the family. Left his wedding ring on the dresser with a note that said he was done. Ever since, Jason has been spinning out of control. He's hurting. Mom doesn't know what to do. She brings him by regularly, and I meet with him in my office. I spend time with him and walk with him through the pain he's experiencing as a young child. He loves to draw and expresses himself through his pictures. We spend time drawing pictures together. I'm honored to be part of his life.

Being a single parent isn't easy, but single parents can still raise great kids. In fact, single parents raised 11 United States presidents. I've watched single parents rise above the challenges. In one church where I served, there was a single mom who was committed to raising her son to serve God. I watched as she lived a Christlike life before him, faithfully brought him to church, and made sure to surround him with good men who invested in his life. Today he's a pastor with a family of his own.

The investment you make in single parents and their preschoolers will make a big difference in their lives. Be intentional about reaching out to them.

—Dale

81

Millennial Parents: What You Need to Know

Born between 1982 and 2000, Millennials are and will be the parents of the preschoolers you're ministering to. As you seek to connect with Millennials, here are important characteristics to know about their generation.

- They were brought up sheltered, coddled, and valued.
- They're confident.
- They're overachieving.
- Their parents paid a lot of attention to them, so they have a sense of entitlement.
- They're team-oriented.
- They're very interested in their children's success.
- They're very educated but anxious.
- They're techno-savvy.
- They have short attention spans. They were MTV-raised.
- They grew up with email. They want an immediate response.
- They were brought up with managed schedules of soccer, school, music lessons, homework, and so on.
- They're diverse and tolerant.
- They're optimistic locally, but pessimistic nationally.
- They have high expectations of authority and institutions.
- They highly value community and are highly relational.
- They want to make a difference.
- They're multi-taskers. The average mom accomplishes the equivalent of 27 hours a day through multi-tasking.

- They're high consumers of media. Each day moms spend 2.6 hours with the Internet, 2.1 hours with TV, 1.2 hours with the radio, and 30 minutes with magazines, newspapers, books, and so on.

- They value having a family. There were more babies born in 2007 than at the height of the baby boom.

- They put their kids ahead of their careers.

- They're interested in healthy, locally grown organic foods.

- They emphasize family experiences over material things. They seek travel and learning experiences.

- They use technology and media to help focus their lives as parents. They reach out to their online families for parenting tips and information.

- They're raising their children with more of a relational approach than an authoritarian approach.

An effective preschool ministry is one that connects and partners with Millennial parents. Here are tips for your preschool ministry drawn from the above characteristics.

- **They grew up with email.** These parents are used to getting an immediate response through texting and cell phones. Return phone calls and emails within 24 hours.

- **They're interested in their preschoolers' success.** Programs such as "Your Baby Can Read" abound. Parents want their children to grow spiritually. Have a clear, focused curriculum pathway and communicate it to parents. Partner with parents and give them tools to extend the weekend lesson into their homes during the week.

- **They want to make a difference.** Get parents involved in their children's experience at church. Give them opportunities to serve in preschool ministry.

- **They use technology and media to help focus their lives as parents.** Create a website and online community for preschool parents in your ministry, or point them to websites that offer parenting tips.

- **They're team-oriented.** Ask for parents' advice and input. Have parent focus groups.

- **They have short attention spans.** They were raised on MTV, so design communication tools that are precise and quick.

- **They're diverse and tolerant.** Create a welcoming environment for everyone in your church. Reflect this throughout your advertising and communication materials.

- **They have high expectations of authority and institutions.** Do things with excellence. Remember they're comparing you to Disneyland and McDonald's.

- **They value community and are highly relational.** They're constantly connected through Facebook, Twitter, email, and cell phones. Create a Facebook page for preschool parents in your ministry. Spend time building relationships with them online and face-to-face.

- **They emphasize family experiences over material things.** Create shared events for preschool families, such as family worship experiences, summer picnics, fall festivals, and "Happy Birthday, Jesus" parties at Christmas.

We have a great opportunity to make a difference in the lives of the Millennial generation and the lives of their preschool children. Take time to study these characteristics with your team. Formulate an effective ministry strategy that will enable you to connect with this new generation of pre-school parents.

—**Dale**

The Proof Is in the Pudding

The number of children in the United States allergic to foods such as peanuts, milk, wheat, and fish is rising rapidly. An estimated 3 million children under the age of 18 had some sort of food allergy in 2007, an 18 percent increase since 1997, according to the U.S. Centers for Disease Control and Prevention. There's been an increase in severe rashes, anaphylaxis (obstruction of the airway), and intestinal problems. Most children react only after eating the foods they're allergic to, but some children will go anaphylactic just by touching the food. These problems are creating a tremendous amount of stress in the homes of those children who are affected by allergies.

As a preschool ministry leader, you need to research childhood allergies so you can provide care for families who have preschoolers suffering from them. Take time to discuss these issues with your preschool staff. It's important that everyone has a full understanding of the problem. Here are suggestions to consider that offer varying degrees of care—from minimum to maximum.

Post snack alerts. *Always* post snack alerts on the doors to your preschool ministry classrooms. It's vitally important that parents know what their children will be snacking on that day.

Use allergy stickers. We place bright red stickers on preschoolers who have mild allergies but still need special care. Each sticker includes the child's name and his or her specific allergy or allergies. This helps volunteers and gives parents peace of mind.

Make your preschool facility a peanut-free zone. We don't allow the children to bring any peanut butter or peanut-related products. We also make sure to serve only peanut-free snacks, which means snacks weren't processed in a facility that uses peanuts. (We also ask parents not to bring milk after their preschoolers reach a certain age. We simply ask parents to bring juice or water.)

Open an allergy room. If you're fortunate enough to have extra space, this might be just the right thing for your preschool ministry. In an allergy room, the teacher is fully aware of each child's needs and can deliver care accordingly. Most children who'd be in the allergy room probably have EpiPens, so an adult in the room needs to be familiar with how to use one. This room should be peanut-free, milk-free, and wheat-free. The only snacks allowed are those that parents bring.

When caring for families whose children have allergies, remember that this is a very stressful time in their lives. They need our patience, love, and understanding. Go the extra mile. Do everything possible to ensure they're getting the best care.

—Gina

83

Working With Adult Ministries

Your ministry to preschoolers' parents is vitally important because when you influence parents, you influence the primary source of spiritual formation in preschoolers.

A partnership with the adult ministries in your church is one of the most strategic moves you can make to leverage the impact of your preschool ministry.

For too long, ministries inside churches have been silos...operating independently of each other. Competing for resources, volunteers, finances, and recognition. It's time to break down those silos and work together as a team to influence families for Christ. Each ministry must see the big picture and realize that it's about reaching the entire family. Take the lead by initiating a partnership with the adult ministries in your church.

- Set up a meeting with the adult team. Share a vision of partnering to reach the entire family. Strategize how you can work together to accomplish this.

- Be aware of parenting and marriage classes that'll help your preschool parents. Find out when these classes are offered and promote them to parents through your take-home papers, emails, posters, and so on.

- Survey your preschool parents. Find out their biggest needs and struggles. Work with adult ministries to offer classes or small groups targeting these issues.

- Be involved with MOPS and women's ministries. Take part in these ministries. Offer to help serve or teach occasionally to build bridges.

- Partner with adult ministries to provide marriage and parenting mentors for young parents of preschoolers. If you're building relationships with the parents of preschoolers, they'll come to you when they're struggling or want to grow in their marriages. Young mothers will come seeking advice on how to navigate the preschool parenting years. Work closely with adult ministries to provide mentors for preschool parents in these areas. Have seasoned married couples who can offer practical advice and counseling. Have experienced parents who've successfully navigated the preschool years ready to come alongside young parents.

- Partner with adult ministries to teach parenting and marriage series for preschool parents. In a few weeks I'll partner with our senior pastor and one of our campus pastors to teach about parenting at our weekend services. The three of us will teach as a team. I'm excited to see what God does with this in our preschool parents' lives.

Make adult ministries your preschool ministry's best friend. You'll see entire families benefit as a result.

—**Dale**

84

We're in This Together

Family devotion times are wonderful and much needed, but they could be a thing of the past. We've found that it's even better when parents talk about God's Word and the things of God as they go about everyday activities with their children. Then and only then do children see God's Word in action.

A modern-day version of Deuteronomy 6:4-9 might go like this: Teach your children about God while you're driving to school, as you're playing ball, while you're waiting at the drive thru, and as you put your children to bed at night.

Here are practical ways your preschool ministry can equip parents with the resources they need to effectively help their children see God's Word in action.

Enlist your pastor's help to equip parents. Once or twice a year on Sunday morning, share your passion for preschool ministry and your desire to help parents better equip their preschoolers for spiritual growth. Have your pastor and other church leaders talk about the creative things they've done in their homes to live out God's Word throughout the day.

Communicate with parents to reinforce Bible learning. Use take-home fliers, newsletters, email, your website, or social networks such as Facebook to let parents know what you're teaching. We do this with every month's lessons. For example, if the monthly verse is Joshua 1:9 and the monthly Bible point is "God wants us to be brave," we encourage parents to use the Bible verse whenever their children experience fear; for example, at bedtime, a doctor's visit, or starting a new school. When preschoolers can hear God's Word and learn to apply it to their everyday lives, they'll "get" it. Parents can't reinforce at home what you're teaching at church if they aren't informed.

Encourage teachers to resource parents. Parents should never leave your preschool ministry empty-handed. Always have teachers give parents take-home resources so they can remind their children about each week's Bible point. Moses said to write God's Word on the doorposts of our houses and on our gates—what about on our refrigerators and our walls? Teachers can say something like, "Didn't Katelyn do a great job on her artwork today? Her Bible verse is at the bottom. Put it on your refrigerator when you get home, and help her with her Bible verse this week."

Do what you have to do to ensure that parents have what they need to help their preschoolers grow spiritually.

—Gina

The Trust Factor

I cringe every time I read of a child who was injured or abused in a church or preschool center. I don't know how I would react if it were my child...I don't even like thinking about it. I constantly remind our staff of the great responsibility we have not only to God but also to the parents who entrust us with the most precious thing on earth to them—their preschoolers. We must go the extra mile to build trust with parents. Here's how.

- Keep rooms clean. When parents look inside preschool ministry rooms, they quickly assess cleanliness. If rooms are untidy, cluttered, or dirty, parents' trust factor will evaporate. Keep toys clean and disinfected, throw away or repair damaged furniture, keep the floor vacuumed and the trash emptied.

- Let parents know every volunteer has been through an orientation process that includes a background check, reference checks, and an interview. Put this information in writing and regularly remind parents. Knowing that you've done due diligence to have only approved volunteers builds trust.

- Let parents know your safety rules. Clearly communicate the rules you've put in place, such as no adult being allowed to be alone with a child.

- Do things with excellence. A commitment to excellence lets parents know you're worthy of their trust. This will be shown not by what you say, but by what you do.

- Follow proper ratios. Nothing will deplete trust more quickly than a parent looking into a room that's too crowded or understaffed.

- Have a secure check-in/check-out system. This is critical to build trust. Parents must know that their preschoolers can't be picked up by anyone else.

- Issue pagers or use on-screen numbers, cell phones, or text messages to notify parents when they're needed. This gives parents a sense of security and helps them feel more comfortable about leaving their preschoolers with you.

- Regularly communicate with parents through newsletters, email, phone, Facebook, and so on. Direct communication about their children's experience at church instills trust. Parents want to know; they want to be involved.

- Fill out incident reports. Preschoolers are going to fall down; they're going to get bumps, scrapes, and scratches. Hardly a week goes by without this happening. The key is how you respond and communicate with parents. Any time there's an accident or incident, write a report that describes exactly what happened. When the parents come to pick up their child, share the incident report with them and have them sign it. This builds trust. Trust is depleted if they go home and discover a bump or scratch they weren't told about.

Trust must be earned. And remember—it only takes seconds to destroy trust. Be diligent to earn parents' trust, week in and week out. As you lead with integrity, their trust in you and your team will grow stronger with each passing year.

—**Dale**

Friday Night Out

Families are under such stress all week that when Sunday morning comes around, many parents think it's easier to roll over and go back to sleep. After all, this is their only day to rest. We took a long hard look at this issue and decided to do something about it.

The idea we came up with is Friday Night Out. Every Friday night we provide free child care for couples. The kicker is that parents attend one of our small groups ahead of time to receive their free child care vouchers.

We offer care for children ages 6 months to fifth grade. This is a win/win for everyone. We have the opportunity of teaching, discipling, and equipping parents through our small group ministry, and in return couples are blessed with 3½ hours of free time on Friday nights. This is marriage enrichment at its best.

Here are guidelines we use to ensure that our program runs as smoothly as possible.

- Each couple must attend a Sunday morning or weekday small group. During this time they'll receive a free child care voucher for the following Friday.

- Every couple must make child care reservations by midnight on the Wednesday prior to the Friday night. We have an email setup that makes child care reservations quick and easy.

- Parents must see that children eat dinner before they're dropped off on Friday nights. We offer child care from 6:00 to 9:30 p.m. and provide a light snack.

- Couples must present their vouchers at drop-off.

- Parents must fill out an accident release form for each child.

How's this been going? I give it an A+. Couples spend more quality time alone together, reconnecting and communicating. We receive emails each week that express gratitude about how Friday Night Out is helping marriages move to new levels of growth. Our prayer is that God will bless homes with newfound peace, love, and joy.

—**Gina**

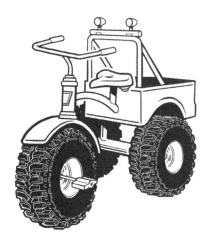

87

Play Days and Away Days

Stay-at-home moms have the toughest job on the planet. Day-to-day activities can get old and tiresome, and I've had moms tell me on occasion how they struggle with deep feelings of aloneness. When I hear words like these, I wish I could gather all the stay-at-home moms in my arms.

Ministry is all about people, and moms are sometimes the most overlooked. Creating a ministry to help young moms not only benefits the mothers in your church, it just might also change the life direction of moms in your surrounding community.

Our church offers "play days" for moms and preschoolers and "away days" for moms once a week during the summer months and once a month during the school year.

- On play days, moms and kids come together to engage in play time or physical activity. We also offer programs such as art days during the summer for preschoolers and their families.

- Away days are days when preschoolers and moms take a break from each other. We offer a Kids Day Out and a Mothers of Preschoolers (MOPS) program to give moms a much needed break. MOPS gives moms time for fellowship, group discussion, and spiritual growth.

Our Kids Day Out program was the front door of our church for one mom with two preschoolers; she was desperate for a break and a weekly opportunity to catch up on hard-to-accomplish tasks. She first heard about Kids Day Out from a neighbor, and eventually she and her husband made faith commitments to Christ. This is a perfect example of how ministering to moms in the community just might change the direction of their lives.

So step back. Take a look at your ministry. Are you meeting the needs of your young mothers? Are you bridging the gap between your preschool ministry and the community of mothers surrounding your church? I can't think of a better way to open the "heart doors" of your church than by taking care of moms. Who knows, you just might see a family changed forever. And that would be a very good thing.

—**Gina**

Preschool Ministry Leadership & Vision

88

Not the Baby Sitters Club

"Give me the child for seven years, and I will give you the man."

—St. Ignatius of Loyola

Ever heard statements like these?

"Is there child care available during the adult service?"

"Wow...I didn't know you actually did all this with the kids during service!"

"I'm glad they have people to watch the kids so I can have a break."

The average person in our churches doesn't understand the vital importance of preschool ministry in helping children become lifelong followers of Christ. They think the kids are cute and assume we sing a few songs and share a Bible story with them, but they don't grasp the strategic vision we have for preschoolers.

How do we shift the mindset of our church members from baby sitters club to strategic ministry? Squeak, squeak, squeak. You know the old saying, "The squeaky wheel gets the oil." It's our job as children's ministers to champion our preschool ministries. Take the lead and let the people in your church know why preschool ministry is so important. If you want to change the baby-sitting mindset, then tell people why it's not baby-sitting!

- **Connect with leadership.** I'm blessed to be in a church that truly values preschool ministry. It's considered one of the key ministries of our church. Not in a situation like this? Then take the initiative. Sit down with your church leaders and, with a humble spirit, talk about the importance of preschool ministry.

- **Share stories.** One of the best things you can do is tell stories about how your ministry impacts preschoolers and their families. Look for opportunities to share. Every Tuesday our church staff meets for faith-sharing and prayer. I enjoy telling stories about how God is working in preschoolers' and their families' lives. This reminds everyone of why we do what we do.

- **Portray the image you want.** Does the name of your preschool ministry reflect your vision, such as Bible Discovery Zone? Are there tag lines you can use to cast vision, such as "Discovering That God Is Everywhere!"?

- **Constantly remind your team that this is ministry, not baby-sitting.** Start with your volunteers. When they grasp the importance of their ministry and get excited about it, they'll spread the word to others.

- **Highlight preschoolers.** Have a children's day once a year where the entire church's attention is turned toward the children's ministry. Let preschoolers have a part in the main service, and use this as an opportunity to share your vision of preschool ministry.

- **Publicize what happens during preschool ministry.** Invite parents to observe preschool ministry. Videotape preschool worship, and play it in your hallways and other key areas in your building. Use take-home papers and bulletin boards to draw attention to what preschoolers are learning.

A church that sees preschool ministry for what it truly is will support it with finances, resources, and people. Very few people want to be part of a baby sitters club at church—but there are lots of people who want to be part of a vital ministry that lays the foundation for children to become lifelong followers of Christ.

—**Dale**

Do You Have a GPS for Your Preschool Ministry?

I'm your typical guy. I won't stop and ask for directions until after I've driven around lost for several hours. It's cost me lots of time and gas over the years. Finally, I wised up and bought a GPS navigator for our car. Now I just type in the destination and this awesome piece of technology calculates the route. It even talks to me along the way and tells me where to turn and how many miles I have left to go. No more wandering around lost with a male ego in the way of getting help.

Lesson learned: If you're going to effectively reach your destination, you need a calculated route. The same is true with your preschool ministry. If you're going to take children to a destination, you need a calculated route to get them there.

Decide on your destination. First, sit down with your team and grapple with these questions:

- Where do we want preschoolers to end up when they transition out of our ministry?

- What do we want them to know and believe about God?

- What key biblical truths do we want them to know and be living out?

- What spiritual growth markers do we want them to reach?

- How will we partner with parents to see all of the above happen? (A first step is to involve parents in working through these questions with you.)

Calculate your route. After you've determined your destination, you're ready for the next steps.

- Decide what curriculum will take kids to what you want them to know and believe about God. What curriculum will communicate the key biblical truths you want children to know? The curriculum should contain Scripture that communicates these truths. The main point is not specific Bible events, but the truths the events illustrate.

- Create evaluation tools to help you measure how preschoolers are living out the biblical truths you want them to know. For example, are they showing kindness by sharing toys? seeking forgiveness by saying they're sorry when they hurt others?

- Design a plan that enables preschoolers to reach the spiritual growth markers you choose.

- Create ways to partner with parents in all these areas through tools such as car tags with questions about each week's Bible point, take-home papers with mealtime discussion starters, and music videos or CDs of worship songs kids are learning.

Time is too precious to let children wander aimlessly through your preschool ministry. Between age 3 and kindergarten, there are only 156 weekends. Don't squander any of them. Every weekend must be part of a calculated route if you're going to see preschoolers arrive at the destination. God wants to use you to guide them each step of the way...helping them navigate toward a strong biblical foundation on which they can build a lifetime of faith.

—Dale

Show Me the Money: Budgeting in Preschool

Budgeting for a preschool ministry presents a unique challenge because of all the age-specific needs. The requirements for ministry to 3-year-olds aren't the same as those for 4-year-olds; the 4-year-olds' requirements are different from the kindergartners'. Your budget needs to be created from multiple points of view because crafts, manipulatives, games, and teaching aids target particular learning stages.

The easiest way to develop this budget is to break it into simple steps. Start with the fundamental questions and needs that you encounter every year.

1. How many children are in this department? Don't forget to look at your church growth statistics and increase the number by that percentage.

2. What are the curriculum needs? What supplies and teaching aids need to be replaced in your curriculum? Is your curriculum age-appropriate? Do you need to purchase new curriculum?

3. How much do you need for supplies and consumables? What do you need to purchase for snacks or food experiences? What do you need for general classroom supplies such as tissue, wipes, and paper towels? What do you need to purchase for crafts? Will you need new toys or props?

4. What do you need for volunteers? Don't forget to budget for small gifts or an appreciation dinner for your volunteers. What training opportunities will you provide?

5. Are you offering special events for your preschoolers? Do you need to budget for VBS? What other special events will you offer for preschoolers?

6. Is your preschool ministry's security/check-in system adequate? What's the cost for upkeep on your current security system?

7. What are your facility needs? Do any of your tables or chairs need replacing? Tables and chairs for 3-year-olds will be a different size than those for 5-year-olds. Make sure your rooms are comfortable for your preschoolers. Do your rooms need paint or decoration?

Once you've answered all these questions and calculated your budget, spend time preparing to present the needs of your ministry. This is as important as the time you've spent preparing the numbers. Remember these important points:

- **Never present a lump sum.** The total amount will appear on the bottom line, but the best way to begin your budget presentation is to show how much you're spending per child, per week.

- **Account for increases since the last budget.** If your budget's increased from the year before, give a clear explanation. For example, is it due to growth, addition of programs, furniture needs? Make your increased needs understandable.

- **Be ready to compromise.** Realize there's always a possibility that your budget will need to be cut. Figure out ahead of time what you can eliminate, and have these numbers ready.

—**Barbara**

Security in a preschool ministry is a concern that's resulted in the release of dozens of books, lectures, training sessions, church consultants, and a huge variety of check-in systems. Many churches, though, especially small ones, feel they're safe from predator dangers. Some churches refuse to consider the possibility that an incident could possibly occur. But an atmosphere of trust, grace, and lack of suspicion leaves a church more susceptible to incidents of abuse or abduction. And, unfortunately, there's no "test" that will identify a possible molester.

So how do you protect your preschoolers? No simple solution guarantees safety. You need a system of checks and balances that provide different aspects of security.

Background checks—The average offender won't attempt to volunteer if he or she is required to fill out a volunteer form. But background checks can give a false sense of security. A background check is really only good for that day; a person could commit a crime the next day, and you wouldn't know it. Make it a habit to randomly select and process previously filed background checks every few months.

The six-month rule—Establish a length of time a person must be a church member, such as six months, before he or she can volunteer to work with preschoolers. Even then, people should begin as assistants and not as lead teachers.

Two-adult rule—Always, always, have two adults in a classroom no matter how small the class size. If the two adults are related, there should also be another adult with them in the preschool room. The age of 18 is generally considered adult, but some churches prefer their teachers to be 21.

Visibility—Have a window or some means of visibility in every classroom and teaching area. Never allow children and teachers behind closed doors.

Diaper changing—Allow diaper changing in one location only, such as your nursery, which is usually staffed with several people. If needed, have extra volunteers walking the halls to take children who need their diapers changed to the nursery. This also ensures that one teacher isn't left alone with preschoolers for any period of time.

Restroom policy—In a preschool department, there's no way to avoid the fact that children will have to be accompanied to the restroom. Even if parents are asked to take their preschoolers to the restroom before class, you need to have a restroom policy and procedure. Most important, make sure that no one teacher or volunteer is allowed to take a child to the restroom unattended. As with diaper changing, have extra staff available to take children to the restroom and then back to class.

Identification verification—The most common threat of abduction in a church setting is from a noncustodial parent. You need a system to identify that the right person is picking up each child. This system can vary from very expensive scan systems to a simple system of matching tags or numbered name tags. However, a church can't enforce a custody agreement unless it's given a copy of the ruling.

Awareness—Last, but not least, keep a watchful eye at all times.

—**Barbara**

Is Your Cup Overflowing?

During the 17 years I've been in preschool ministry, I've had great years and not-so-great years, but I've learned the key to staying fresh and tapping into God's unending resources. For me it begins with the simple idea that I've got to have it before I can give it. When I get to my wits' end, when I feel tired, weary, and maybe even angry, I have to go back and ask myself this simple question: *How's my time with God going?*

I confess that there were years when I lost my time with God. I excused myself because I had so much to do *for* God. These were important things, but I was doing them with an empty soul. It didn't take long until I came to the end of my rope. I was exhausted, empty, angry, and burned out. At this pivotal time in my life, I made a commitment to spend time daily with God. As a servant of Christ in his local church, I had to understand that this discipline was a nonnegotiable.

If this describes you, I pray you'll make a commitment to begin again. We were never meant to bear this burden alone. The yoke we put on ourselves is never easy to bear, never light. Taking this burden off is a daily discipline. Each morning God waits for us to enter his presence; he anticipates our worship and longs to ease our burdens for the day. Why would any of us pass this up?

We have the opportunity to touch many lives each week. We can fake it for only so long, and then our cup empties. We dry up and are no longer able to pour our lives into the lives of others. This is tragic and all too common in ministry life. I don't know about you, but I want to be so full of Jesus that when I bump into people throughout the day, I spill Jesus all over them.

Our cups can remain full. We can be ready to pour the very life Jesus has given us into others at any given moment. That's living the Christian life to its fullest. Determine for yourself today that this one discipline, the habit of spending time alone in the presence of God, will be a nonnegotiable for you.

—**Gina**

Envision Your Preschool Ministry

A compelling vision communicates that kingdom impact is happening in the lives of preschoolers and that you're laying the biblical foundation for their spiritual growth. Establishing a vision for your preschool ministry is essential to knowing where you're going and getting everyone on the same page to get there.

Vision determines direction. It's nearly impossible to get where you're going without the ability to see where you're going. Not knowing where you're going is like navigating your way through a room with a blindfold on. A vision for your preschool ministry helps you clarify what you want and how to get there. It opens your eyes to the possibilities.

Vision facilitates decision making. If you know where you're headed, you can say no to things that won't help you get there and yes to those things that will. Vision gives you the focus to see the end goal and avoid the obstacles that will keep you from reaching it.

Vision creates alignment. Not long ago, I was driving down the road and noticed that my car was pulling to the left. Every time I took my hands off the wheel, my car veered toward the centerline. I took my car to the mechanic and he told me that the front end was "out of alignment." He told me that misalignment could cause major problems if I didn't get it fixed. Well, I got it fixed and now my car is running smoothly.

The same thing is true of our ministries. If we're out of alignment, it can cause major problems. In preschool ministry, vision creates alignment. It becomes a rallying point and puts everyone on the same page, working together to accomplish the same goals.

Vision communicates a clear message. A compelling vision presents a clear message to your church, your volunteers, and your preschoolers' parents about what you want to see happen in the lives of the children and families. When people understand the vision of your ministry, it becomes a shared vision that enables everyone to work together to make it happen.

One final note about vision: Only *you* can determine the vision of your preschool ministry. Please don't misunderstand that statement. You'll need to work with your senior pastor and your church staff to make sure your vision is synchronized with the overall vision of the church. But you have to determine what you want to see happen in the lives of preschoolers and then design a plan to make it happen.

—Eric

Your preschool ministry is a barometer of the health of your church because a healthy church reaches young families. I'm thankful for our church's seniors, and I look to them for wisdom, insight, and encouragement—our churches should be ministering to them as well. A healthy church will reach all generations. But if your church is primarily gray, then the barometer indicates things aren't healthy.

In Florida we have a lot of seniors, especially in the winter months. When snowbirds migrate down at the beginning of winter, semis full of snowbirds' cars start arriving. Soon afterward you begin to see "silver alerts" on electronic highway signs. A silver alert means a senior driver who has dementia or Alzheimer's disease has been reported missing and may cause major safety issues on the road. Information about the make and model of the car flashes on the sign.

Look around your church—is there a silver alert, or is there a good percentage of young families with preschoolers? If gray hair is all you see, how do you increase your church's health?

Church members must be willing to change. All across our country there are small churches made up of older families who are unwilling to change. These churches aren't reaching young families because church members are determined to keep a church culture from the 1960s. I've served in contemporary churches that were full of young families. I've had conversations with some of the older members. How did they adjust to the loud music? How did they handle the change over the years? I've always received the same response: "It's not about us. It's about reaching the next generation of families." Wow! No wonder their churches are healthy and full of preschool families.

The senior pastor and leadership must be committed to reaching young families. Everything rises and falls on leadership. Leaders must be willing to appeal to young families. The top two questions people ask when they pick a church are (1) How friendly are you? and (2) What do you have to offer my kids?

The church must make preschool ministry a top priority. Finances, resources, and staffing must walk this talk.

Church greeters and ushers should include preschool parents. When preschool parents walk in the doors of your church, who greets them? Are any of them people their own age?

Sit down with your team and rate the health of your church based on the percentage of preschool families that attend. What does the barometer say? Do you need to formulate an action plan to increase your church's health?

—**Dale**

95

Planning Your Priorities

The tasks required to make preschool ministry happen can be daunting. Over the years I've been blessed with opportunities to watch, listen, and learn from great leaders who amazed me with what they were able to accomplish. Here's what's helped me most along the way.

Plan your work and work your plan. This one concept has helped me more than anything else in the area of organization and productivity. Every Sunday, I take a half-hour to go over my workweek and write down what I'd like to accomplish. Then I break it into daily bite-size tasks. I plan my time with God, workouts, lunches with leaders, writing thank you notes—everything. When you do this, you'll be amazed at what you can get done.

Daily and weekly tasks can be all-consuming, yet even harder are those ministry projects and programs that take months to plan and carry out. Stop and ask yourself these two questions: *What's best for the ministry? What will help us fulfill our mission statement?* At the end of the day, you must be able to say that your programs, projects, and plans fit into God's ultimate plan for your ministry. When I have several options in front of me, I take heed of Christian author Elisabeth Elliot's advice and ask God, "What's next?" Then I quiet myself and listen. Amazingly, God shows me what to do.

Know what to give and what to keep. A good leader delegates; an insecure leader keeps everything for her- or himself. Have you ever known people who won't give things away? They're usually stressed and overworked, with little time for family and life outside of ministry. It's important to have a team that helps you carry the burden of ministry. It's equally important that you play to their strengths and give them the right tasks.

Also, recognize and honor those things that you need to hold on to, things that you and you alone can do. Define this for yourself, and give everything else to team leaders who share your vision, passion, and desire to see ministry move forward.

—Gina

Building Blocks

My dad was a contractor, so I've been around construction sites my entire life. One thing my dad always taught me was that the success of the building was determined by its foundation. A strong foundation equals a strong building; a weak foundation equals a weak building.

Whether you're building a house, your life, or a preschool ministry, the same principle applies. If you want to be successful, you have to start with the right foundation. When it comes to building a preschool ministry, I've identified two building blocks that determine success.

Transformational truth—The first building block of a successful preschool ministry is found in the Great Commandment. The transformational truth that we build our preschool ministries on is *love*. It begins when we love God. We put God first in everything we do; then based on our love for God, we're able to love ourselves. This means we teach preschoolers that the choices they make matter. All of their choices have either good or bad consequences. The decisions we make in life move us closer to God or further away from God. When we properly love God and love ourselves, then we can properly love others. This means we also teach preschoolers that the way we treat other people matters and that we need to look out for the interests of others.

As preschoolers learn to love God, love themselves, and love others, God will begin to change them from the inside out.

Relational connections—The second building block of a successful preschool ministry is the relational connections we create.

- **We connect with parents.** The key here is partnership. We come alongside parents and work together to help their preschoolers develop a relationship with Jesus. We provide them with tools and resources to help them guide their preschoolers on their spiritual journey.

- **We connect with volunteers.** The key here is teamwork. Realize that every volunteer has a role to play in the spiritual formation of preschoolers. We also need to design ways for volunteers to build relationships with each other. To build an effective team with our volunteers, we need to create a culture of trust.

- **We connect with preschoolers.** The key here is relevance. Our lessons, songs, crafts, and activities need to be relevant to preschoolers. They need to be age-appropriate and connect with kids on their level. Every week our preschoolers need to learn the Bible in a fun, engaging environment.

Every builder knows that the right foundation is fundamental to the success of each building. As we instill in our preschoolers love for God, themselves, and others and connect with parents, volunteers, and kids, we'll be well on our way to designing a preschool ministry that stands the test of time.

—Eric

Boo-Boos, Bumps, and Bruises

In a preschool department, injuries will happen. To make sure that every injury is handled in the best possible way, every staff member and volunteer needs to know the correct safety procedures. We place large posters in every room that give step-by-step instructions for what to do in an emergency. Here are the posters' basic guidelines, plus suggestions for adapting a first-aid kit to your preschoolers' needs:

Stop and think. The first thing to do is to stop, look at the situation, and answer these questions:

Is the child unresponsive?

Is the child having difficulty breathing?

Is the child's cry unusual?

Don't panic. Panic is extremely contagious, spreading in a matter of seconds and adding chaos to an already bad situation. Evaluate the situation and the answers to the questions above, and then decide what to do. If you're not sure what to do, seek assistance.

Locate the first-aid kit. A first-aid kit in a church should be readily available, well-stocked, and clearly labeled. If you've purchased a first-aid kit, it likely includes many items that are inadequate for the needs of preschoolers. Make these changes to adapt your kit:

- Replace adult-size bandages with kid-friendly character bandages in small sizes.

- Replace adult medications with children's medications. *Note of warning: Never dispense medication.* You may have it available, but a parent or a doctor should be the only one who ever dispenses medication.

- Replace ice packs with child-size boo-boo packs, which are available in most drugstores and usually designed around popular cartoon characters.

• Butterfly closures need to be cut and overlapped to work for a child, so make sure a small set of scissors is available.

• Add a battery-operated ear thermometer.

In case of emergency, use this call list. A list of emergency numbers by the first-aid kit and the nearest phone needs to include these numbers: doctors and nurses who attend your church, the local hospital emergency department, poison control, and the fire department.

Fill out an injury report. Any time a child is injured at church and requires any medical attention, fill out a report in duplicate. One is given to the parent; one is filed in the church office. This report needs to include information about the child, the date and time of the accident, how the child was injured, action that was taken to treat the injury, and a list of names and phone numbers of adults who witnessed the injury. Parents, the teacher, and the director need to sign both copies of the report.

—**Barbara**

Keep Dreaming

Proverbs 29:18 (NASB) says, "Where there is no vision, the people are unrestrained." When I think of the word *unrestrained*, I think of complete chaos. Maybe your ministry is unrestrained or in a state of chaos right now. Could it be for lack of vision? That's a tough question to ask, but one that must be addressed. Here's what you need to know about vision for your ministry.

God is the giver of great vision. And God alone instills in us the passion for what we do. If you're struggling, you need to go back to your calling. Go to the very moment God called you, and ask yourself, *What compelled me to ministry?* I once heard a pastor say, "If you want to know your passion, find out what makes you angry."

In my tenure, God has birthed many new ideas in my heart and mind—some that took years to fulfill. Nothing is more exciting to me than for God to do exceedingly, abundantly beyond all I could ever ask or think. I love it when a dream or vision comes to complete fruition.

However, we can't stop there. We can't sit down, fold our hands, and say the work we've set out to accomplish is done. We must pull ourselves back up and dream again. This is what creative ministry is all about. We need to constantly be reaching, learning, and seeking new ways to effectively reach preschoolers and their families.

Our ministries will only grow as deep and wide as our God-given vision. When our vision is small, our ministry will be small. If, however, our vision expands even beyond what we're capable of doing, we'll be amazed at what God will do.

Once we're clear on our vision, it's imperative that we share it with our teams. It's not uncommon for a leader to share his or her heart, vision, and dreams for the ministry and for one or two team members to completely miss it. With all due respect, if this happens to you, those team members need to step down. God has called you to lead your ministry. He's instilled the vision and dream in your heart. You need a team that'll go the distance with you. When all these elements fall into place, the foundation of your ministry will grow wider and deeper than you ever imagined. And the impact of your ministry will reach far beyond what you thought possible.

So dream, re-dream, and dream again.

—**Gina**

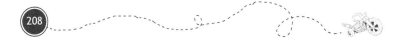

99

The Administrative Blues

Every preschool ministry leader has aspired to his or her position out of love and a desire to change young lives through the Word of God. Most likely you worked as a volunteer for years, gaining experience and training by being a vital part of a children's ministry. Then the great day arrived when you got paid for doing a job you'd have gladly done for free. Even though the weight of responsibility is heavy on your shoulders, it's a burden you bear with joy as you watch a ministry blossom under your supervision.

Unfortunately, you may find yourself bogged down in administration and overwhelmed by policymaking, budgeting, meetings, curriculum, and volunteer management. You wanted to work with children, but instead you're struggling to get your job done and spend time with your family. What's happened? Those creative juices that used to flow freely have gone deep underground, and you find yourself slipping into survival mode ministry. There's no cure for the "administrative blues," but these simple steps can help you continue to enjoy ministry.

Keep your eyes on the children. Preschoolers require a different level of attention than elementary children because of issues such as separation anxiety, contagious crying, and even restroom or diaper situations. It's easy to lose focus and become overwhelmed with running your department, but don't let leadership keep you from living out the child side of your dedication.

You once were an active teacher of preschoolers and worked with them one-on-one. Make a point to engage in preschool ministry with different age groups at least three months a year. It'll keep you refreshed, give you insight into your curriculum, and allow you to build relationships with preschoolers. If you can't find the time to do this, rethink your delegation strategy.

Keep in touch with your leadership. Many church leaders don't realize the details involved in a children's minister's job. It's up to you to keep them informed of the changes or challenges you're facing. They need to know when you're feeling overwhelmed. Seek their wisdom, and don't be afraid to ask for help.

Don't overcommit yourself. This is much easier said than done because of the numerous demands on your time and the great ideas you want to pursue, but you must learn to say no. Not every opportunity is worthwhile.

Make time for creative and physical outlets. We all have something that decompresses our tension. It's necessary to identify what works for you and commit to keeping yourself spiritually, mentally, and physically refreshed.

Take your vacation time. Use the vacation time you're given, and take it in blocks of time, not a day here and a day there. One day off will not give you the break you need and deserve.

Pray and study. God has placed you as a leader for a reason. Keep in constant relationship with him through prayer and by reading the Bible. A prayer journal is a wonderful way to keep yourself disciplined and to express your prayers in a tangible way. A journal also lets you look back to see how God has answered your prayers.

—**Barbara**

100

Lead Like a Preschooler

Leadership can make or break our preschool ministries. To be effective leaders, we need to take some cues from the preschoolers we lead. By matching our leadership with preschoolers' key characteristics, we can take our ministries to the next level.

Choose curiosity over apathy. First of all, preschoolers are naturally curious. Spend longer than 30 seconds with a 4-year-old and you soon realize that they question *everything*. They're extremely inquisitive. They want to explore, discover, and learn.

As a leader, apathy will kill your curiosity and take away your ability to be innovative. If you're apathetic you can't come up with new ideas and creative solutions to the problems you face in ministry. Apathetic leaders conform to the way things are. Curious leaders ask questions such as "Why?" and "What if...?" to discover what can be. They challenge the status quo and explore new ways of doing things.

Choose adaptation over stagnation. Preschoolers adapt to their surroundings. I watch this happen every Sunday as new kids enter our preschool ministry. They may be reluctant at first, but it doesn't take long before they've settled into their new environment. Their fear of the unknown may slow them down, but it doesn't stop them in their tracks. They have an uncanny ability to change and adapt.

Your ability to change and adapt will determine your effectiveness as a leader. Our ministries become stagnant when we refuse to change. Most of us are reluctant when we face changes, but fear of change turns our reluctance into resistance. When we resist change, it stops us in our tracks. Instead choose to embrace change and adapt to it.

Choose risks over retreat. Preschoolers are constantly making progress. They're maturing, growing, and developing. Preschoolers don't retreat from challenges but take risks to solve their dilemmas. The notion "it can't be done" isn't in preschoolers' minds. They'll use their imagination to make the impossible possible. You'll rarely, if ever, find an idle preschooler. They have two speeds...they're either going full steam ahead or they're sleeping.

Leaders make progress. Leaders don't back down from challenges; they creatively figure out ways to overcome them. One of the most common reasons we retreat from a challenge is to avoid failure. Because we don't want to fail, we allow the notion "it can't be done" to become commonplace in our thinking. We avoid the necessary risks that would make our ministry to preschoolers better. Taking calculated risks in our ministries is what makes great things possible. Without taking risks, we can't make improvements in our ministries. Without improvements, we're not making progress.

To become great leaders in our preschool ministries, we need to learn from those we lead, choosing curiosity over apathy, adaptation over stagnation, and risks over retreat. As we allow these preschool characteristics to infiltrate our leadership style, we'll begin to see God lift our ministries to new heights. Our questions will bring clarity, our adaptation to change will melt away our fears, and our risks will open up new ways of doing preschool ministry. So begin today to lead...like a preschooler.

—**Eric**

About the Authors

Eric Echols is the children's pastor at 12Stone Church in Lawrenceville, Georgia, where he serves as the directional leader for over 1,500 children in the nursery, preschool, and elementary ministries. He's actively involved in providing leadership, consulting, and training for children's leaders in the local church. Eric and his wife, Nicole, live in Dacula, Georgia, with their three children, Samuel, Emma, and Wil.

Gina Franzke is director of preschool/women's ministry at First Baptist Church in Springdale, Arkansas, where she's served for 17 years. She has a bachelor's degree in family studies and child development from Southern Nazarene University in Bethany, Oklahoma. Her passion to put the Word of God into the hearts of preschoolers is the driving force in her life. She and her husband, Ed, have two daughters, Meredith, 12, and Katelyn, 8.